Mother Goose and Friends
A Number Activity Book

by Becky Daniel

illustrated by Cara H. Bradshaw

One, two, a book for you;
Three, four, counting and more;
Five, six, seven and eight;
Say, this book is really great!
Nine, ten, eleven and twelve, too,
Have fun with Mother Goose; there's lots to do!

Teaching & Learning Company
1204 Buchanan St., P.O. Box 10
Carthage, IL 62321

Cover by Cara H. Bradshaw

Copyright © 1995, Teaching & Learning Company

ISBN No. 1-57310-011-0

Printing No. 98765432

Teaching & Learning Company
1204 Buchanan St., P.O. Box 10
Carthage, IL 62321

TLC10011 Copyright © Teaching & Learning Company, Carthage, IL 62321

This book belongs to

_____

Table of Contents

TLC10011 Copyright © Teaching & Learning Company, Carthage, IL 62321

1 one

Who is going round my sheep-
    fold?
Only poor old Jacky Lingo.
Don't steal any of my black sheep.
No, no more I will, only by one,
Up, says Jacky Lingo.

Yankee Doodle went to town
Upon a little pony;
He stuck one feather in his hat,
And called it Macaroni.

Sew-saw, sacradown, sacradown,
Which is the way to London town?
One foot up, and the other foot down,
That is the way to London town.

Deedle, deedle, dumpling, my son John,
Went to bed with his stockings on;
One shoe off, and one shoe on,
Deedle, deedle, dumpling, my son John.

Twinkle, twinkle, little star,
How I wonder what you are!
Up above the world so high,
Like a diamond in the sky.

Little Jack Horner
Sat in a corner,
Eating a Christmas pie;
He put in his thumb,
And pulled out one plum,
And said, "What a good boy am I"

Marching to London Town

Sew-saw, sacradown, sacradown,
Which is the way to London town?
One foot up, and the other foot down,
That is the way to London town.

Marching is a good way to teach children to keep time to a beat. Practice marching to the count of one, one, one, one. Stand in a large circle and march in place. Say the rhyme as the children march to the beat of each word. After the children have mastered marching in time, choose a leader to head the line and lead the children around the classroom or playground. Try marching to the other number one rhymes below.

Yankee Doodle went to town
Upon a little pony;
He stuck one feather in his hat,
And called it Macaroni.

Deedle, deedle, dumpling, my son
*   John,*
Went to bed with his stockings on;
One shoe off, and one shoe on,
Deedle, deedle, dumpling, my son
*   John.*

One Delicious Center

*Little Jack Horner
Sat in a corner,
Eating a Christmas pie;
He put in his thumb,
And pulled out one plum,
And said, "What a good boy am I!"*

Getting Ready: Practice life skills with a kitchen center. A kitchen center is easy to assemble and usually provides a great deal of excitement and learning. Food is motivating! Place measuring supplies, one picture recipe and foods needed to complete the dish in the learning center. It is most convenient if the center is located near a sink for easy cleanup. All sessions in the kitchen should begin with the washing of hands and end with washing of supplies and cleaning of the work area. The kitchen center should have a flat work surface and a cutting board. Change the recipe every few days or each week. (See reproducible picture recipes on pages 20-25.) After you have used a few of the picture recipes in the kitchen center, you will be able to create your own easy-to-follow picture directions for creating quick, nutritious snacks. Children can also create picture recipes for the center. Recipes you use will vary depending on the equipment available and the sophistication of your group. If your group has a snack at mid-morning, you may want to let them make their own in the kitchen center each day.

Equipment in center might include:
measuring spoons and cups
hand mixer
bowls
toaster
microwave
refrigerator
liquid detergent
paper towels
sponge for cleanup
paper plates
paper cups
serrated, plastic knives
hand juicer
serving spoons and spatula
baking pans

Learning Center

Peanut Butter and Jelly Pinwheels

Makes 4 tiny sandwiches.

1. Cut crust off one piece of (bread).

2. Roll flat with a (rolling pin).

3. Spread with (peanut) butter.

4. Add (jelly) or jam.

5. Roll up and slice.

Tuna Sandwich

Makes 1 sandwich.

1. In a bowl, stir 1 tablespoon (15 ml) mayonnaise and 2 tablespoons (30 ml) (tuna).

2. On a cutting board, chop $1/2$ stalk of (celery).

3. Add to (tuna).

4. Add 1 tablespoon (15 ml) (pickle) relish.

5. Toast 2 slices of (bread).

6. Put (tuna) on one slice of toast and put other slice of toast on top.

One Baked Potato

1. Wash ⬭ (potato). Poke holes in peel.
2. Place in a ▭ (glass dish).
3. Cook in ▣ (microwave) 3 minutes.
4. Poke with a fork to see if it is done. (If not done, cook another minute.)
5. Remove from oven. Slice open. Top with ▱ (butter).

One Little Pizza

1. Split open an ⬭ (English muffin) and brown in ⬭ (toaster).
2. Spread 1 tablespoon (15 ml) pizza sauce on muffin.
3. Grate cheese.
4. Put grated cheese on sauce.
5. Melt in ▣ (microwave) 30 seconds.

One Waffle

1. Remove frozen (waffle) from package.

2. Toast in (toaster).

3. Top with (butter).

4. Add (jelly) or (syrup).

One Deviled Egg

1. Peel 1 hard-boiled (egg).
2. Cut in half.
3. Remove yolk, place in bowl and mash.
4. Add 1 teaspoon (5 ml) (salad dressing). Stir.
5. Place mixture back in egg white.

Oatmeal

Makes 1 serving.

1. Fill a cup ³/₄ full of water.
2. Add 4 tablespoons (60 ml) (oatmeal).
3. Cover. Cook in (microwave) 2 minutes.
4. Stir. Cook another minute.
5. Add (milk) and sugar.

One Graham Cracker Sandwich

1. Break a (graham cracker) in half.
2. Spread (peanut) butter on both halves or use cake frosting.
3. Add (raisins) or sliced fruit.
4. Make a sandwich.

Learning Center

Apple Sandwiches

1. Wash apple.
2. Cut in half vertically.
3. Cut in quarters horizontally. Remove seeds and core.
4. Spread with (peanut) butter or cream cheese.
5. Add (raisins).

Cheese and Crackers

1. Place 6 (crackers) on plate.
2. On cutting board, slice 3 pieces of cheese.
3. Put (cheese) on 3 crackers.
4. Top each with another (cracker).

Jacky Lingo

Who is going round my sheepfold?
Only poor old Jacky Lingo.
Don't steal any of my black sheep.
No, no more I will, only by one,
Up, says Jacky Lingo.

Getting Ready: Hold hands, the children make a large circle and sit down.

Directions: One child is chosen to be Jacky Lingo, he stands on the outside of the circle. Another child is "It," and she stands inside the circle. "It" asks, "Who is going round my sheepfold?" Jacky Lingo replies, "Only poor old Jacky Lingo." "It" replies, "Don't steal any of my black sheep." And Jacky Lingo says, "No, no more I will, only by one. Up, says Jacky Lingo." When he says, "Up, says Jacky Lingo," he touches a child who stands up and grabs hold of Jacky's waist from the back with both hands. They circle the outside ring of children. Then Jacky Lingo tags another child. The three of them circle the outside of the ring reciting the verse again. Continue playing until all of the children have been gathered. Then "It" chases the train of children and drags off the last child in line to a wall or tree where he must stay. "It" keeps gathering her "black sheep," (children) one at a time, until she has caught and recovered them all.

Choral Readings with Solos

Begin this lesson by explaining to the children that *solo* means "alone or one." Review the number one. Ask the students to name something that they do solo (alone). Then recite the rhymes below as choral readings. Give each individual the opportunity to recite solo lines.

Girls:	*Who is going round my sheepfold?*
Boys:	*Only poor old Jacky Lingo.*
Girls:	*Don't steal any of my black sheep.*
Boys:	*No, no more I will, only by one,*
Solo:	*Up, says Jacky Lingo.*
All:	*Sew-saw, sacradown, sacradown,*
Solo:	*Which is the way to London town?*
All:	*One foot up, and the other foot down,*
	That is the way to London town.
All:	*Yankee Doodle went to town*
All:	*Upon a little pony;*
All:	*He stuck one feather in his hat,*
Solo:	*And called it Macaroni.*
Girl Solo:	*Deedle, deedle, dumpling, my son John,*
Boy Solo:	*Went to bed with his stockings on;*
All:	*One shoe off, and one shoe on,*
Girl Solo:	*Deedle, deedle, dumpling, my son John.*
All:	*Twinkle, twinkle, little star,*
Solo:	*How I wonder what you are!*
All:	*Up above the world so high,*
	Like a diamond in the sky.

Dramatic Play

Deedle, Deedle, Dumpling, My Son John

Practice the rhyme until everyone knows it. Then give each child one word or phrase from the rhyme. (See the large print version of rhyme below and on the next page.) Cut apart the words so that you have as many word cards as there are children in your group. Read each child's word(s) to him. The object is for the children to organize themselves and stand holding their word card so that the words on the cards are sequential. Because the first and last lines of the verse are the same, the children holding these word cards will have to cooperate and make a decision whether to stand at the beginning or end of the line. In the beginning, you may want to work with one sentence at a time. See how quickly the students can assemble themselves with the verse in sequence. Then mix up the cards and have students assemble themselves in order once again.

Variation: After children are assembled in sequential order, have them read their own card aloud. The object is to say the verse with a smooth rhythm as one voice.

Deedle, deedle,

dumpling,

my son John,

Went to bed

with his stockings on;

One shoe off,

and one shoe on,

Deedle, deedle,

dumpling,

my son John.

2 two

There were two birds sat upon a stone,
Fal de ral-al de ral-laddy.
One flew away, and then there was one,
Fal de ral-al de ral-laddy.
The other flew after, and then there was none,
Fal de ral-al de ral-laddy.
So the poor stone was left all alone,
Fal de ral-al de ral-laddy.
One of these little birds back again flew,
Fal de ral-al de ral-laddy.
The other came after, and then there were two,
Fal de ral-al de ral-laddy.
Says one to the other, pray how do you do?
Fal de ral-al de ral-laddy.
Very well, thank you, and pray how are you?
Fal de ral-al de ral-laddy.

There were two blackbirds
Sitting on a hill.
The one named Jack,
And the other named Jill.
Fly away, Jack!
Fly away, Jill!
Come again, Jack!
Come again, Jill!

2 two

Come to the window,
My baby, with me,
And look at the stars
That shine on the sea!
There are two little stars
That play at bo-peep
With two little fish
Far down in the deep;
And two little frogs
Cry neap, neap, neap;
I see a dear baby
That should be asleep.

Little Betty Blue,
Lost her holiday shoe.
What will poor Betty do?
Why, give her another,
To match the other,
And then she will walk in two.

Fly Away, Birds!

There were two blackbirds
Sitting on a hill.
The one named Jack,
And the other named Jill.
Fly away, Jack!
Fly away, Jill!
Come again, Jack!
Come again, Jill!

Count to two. Show the children two fingers. Count them aloud. Talk about how many two are. Recite the rhyme using hands folded like the letter **V** to represent two blackbirds. Use the knees as the hill. Open and close the fingers of both hands to represent flapping bird wings, and move them off the knees and into the air at appropriate times. If children put a lot of action and rhythm into it, this is a good hand and arm exercise.

Variation: You can turn this rhyme into a delightful short play. You will need a narrator and chorus of voices. Let pairs of children take turns playing the blackbirds. Use the whole arms to be birds' wings, and "fly" at appropriate times in the rhyme. (See costume hints on page 46.)

Narrator:	*There were two birds sat upon a stone,*
Chorus:	*Fal de ral-al de ral-laddy.*
Narrator:	*One flew away, and then there was one,*
Chorus:	*Fal de ral-al de ral-laddy.*
Narrator:	*The other flew after, and then there was none,*
Chorus:	*Fal de ral-al de ral-laddy.*
Narrator:	*So the poor stone was left all alone,*
Chorus:	*Fal de ral-al de ral-laddy.*
Narrator:	*One of these little birds back again flew,*
Chorus:	*Fal de ral-al de ral-laddy.*
Narrator:	*The other came after, and then there were two,*
Chorus:	*Fal de ral-al de ral-laddy.*
Narrator:	*Says one to the other, pray how do you do?*
Chorus:	*Fal de ral-al de ral-laddy.*
Narrator:	*Very well, thank you, and pray how are you?*
Chorus:	*Fal de ral-al de ral-laddy.*

Craft

Blackbird Stick Puppets

There were two blackbirds
Sitting on a hill.
The one named Jack,
And the other named Jill.
Fly away, Jack!
Fly away, Jill!
Come again, Jack!
Come again, Jill!

To make blackbird puppets and a stand-up puppet stage, you will need a file folder, two craft sticks and patterns on this page and the following page.

Reproduce the hill pattern on green construction paper. Cut out hill and attach it to the front of a file folder so that when the folder is open it will stand on its own. Reproduce blackbird patterns on white construction paper. Cut out birds. Color them. Attach a craft stick to each one. Use bird puppets and hill to recite the rhyme.

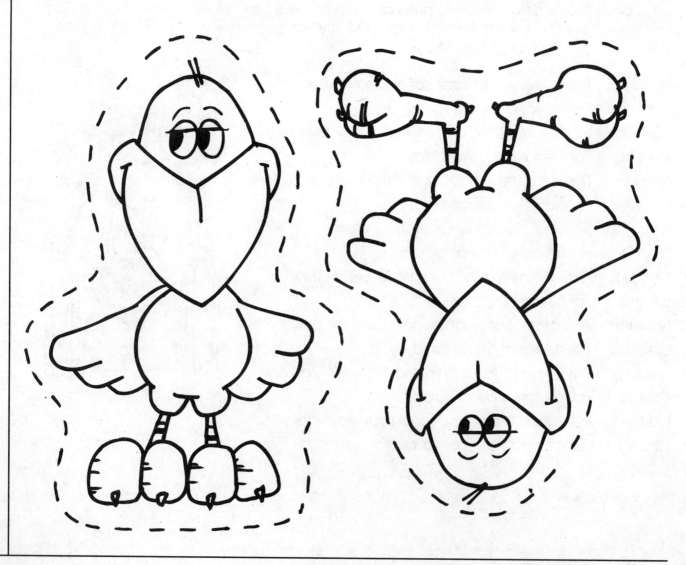

TLC10011 Copyright © Teaching & Learning Company, Carthage, IL 62321

Blackbird Stick Puppets

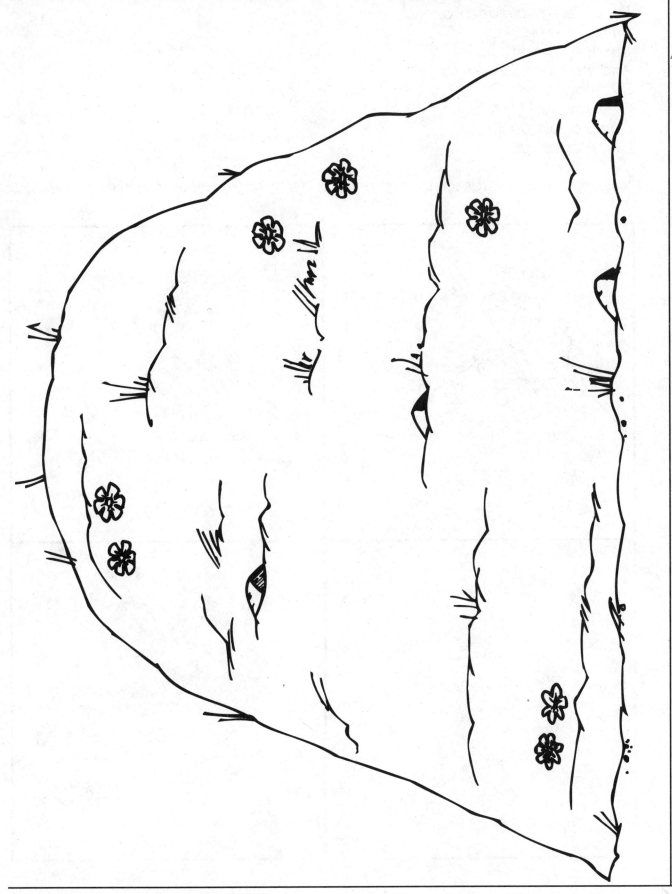

Two Blackbirds

There were two blackbirds
Sitting on a hill.
The one named Jack,
And the other named Jill.
Fly away, Jack!
Fly away, Jill!
Come again, Jack!
Come again, Jill!

Count the blackbirds sitting on the hill. Write the correct number in each box.

A Perfect Match

Little Betty Blue,
Lost her holiday shoe.
What will poor Betty do?
Why, give her another,
To match the other,
And then she will walk in two.

Getting Ready: Collect old pairs of canvas shoes. The more colors and sizes you can collect, the better. Wash and bleach them in the washing machine to make sure they are clean and free of germs. Let dry. Place them in a large box in the center.

Objective: Children are to line up the matching shoes.

Variation: Cut pictures of shoes from books and magazines. Mount each shoe on light cardboard and cut out. Students pair up the pictures of matching shoes. You can use fabric markers to write on the shoes and decorate them.

TLC10011 Copyright © Teaching & Learning Company, Carthage, IL 62321

Puzzle

Two Blackbirds

There were two blackbirds
Sitting on a hill.
The one named Jack,
And the other named Jill.
Fly away, Jack!
Fly away, Jill!
Come again, Jack!
Come again, Jill!

Here are two puzzle pieces. Fit them together to make a picture.

Two Little Stars

Come to the window,
My baby, with me,
And look at the stars
That shine on the sea!
There are two little stars
That play at bo-peep
With two little fish
Far down in the deep;
And two little frogs
Cry neap, neap, neap;
I see a dear baby
That should be asleep.

Directions: Cut out and paste two stars in the sky and two fish in the sea.

2

Pen-Point Twos

This project will demonstrate to the children that the primary colors blue and yellow make green. Pointillism is a method of making new colors by combining tiny points of pure colors. You many choose to use the term with the children or simply say that you are coloring with pen points. Each student will need a blue and yellow fine-tip marker and a copy of the numeral two pattern below. Instead of coloring the numeral with one color, have the children equally mix blue and yellow dots of color. Let them discover that the mixture of these two colors will make green. Complete the picture by outlining the numeral in black. If children enjoy the project, let them experiment by combining the other primary colors: red and blue or red and yellow.

Blackbird Tag

There were two blackbirds
Sitting on a hill.
The one named Jack,
And the other named Jill.
Fly away, Jack!
Fly away, Jill!
Come again, Jack!
Come again, Jill!

Getting Ready: This is a tag game for three people and should be played out-of-doors. Divide children into groups of three. In each group, two of the children are to be the blackbirds. They find a spot to stand.

Directions: The third child is "It." He sings the rhyme. At the appropriate time in the song, the two "blackbirds" fly away. When "It" says, "Come again, Jack!" and "Come again, Jill!" the "blackbirds" try to return to their spot without being tagged. The "blackbirds" use each other to divert the attention of "It." If one of the blackbirds reaches the original spot without being tagged, she gets to be "It."

Dramatic Play

Two Little Birds

Let everyone make his own simple bird costume and turn both of the bird rhymes into
short plays. See play directions on page 37.
Black pants and black shirts can be worn
with wings.

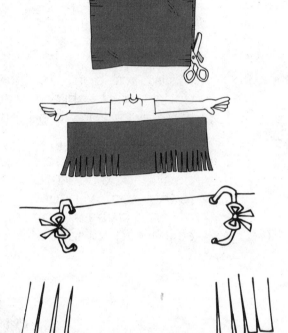

Directions for Making Blackbird Wings

1. Trim off the bottom of a large, black
   trash bag. Cut open the sides. This
   will leave two large rectangles for
   making two sets of wings.

2. Trim rectangles to be exactly as long
   as a student's outstretched arms.
   Fringe one long edge of the rectangles as illustrated.

3. Use a hole punch to put four holes 12"
   (30.48 cm) apart in the center of the
   unfringed edge and tie yarn through
   each hole. Use the yarn to secure the
   wings to the upper part of arms as
   illustrated.

4. Punch two holes in the ends of wings.
   Tie yarn through these holes, too.
   Secure the ends of the wings to each
   wrist with yarn as illustrated.

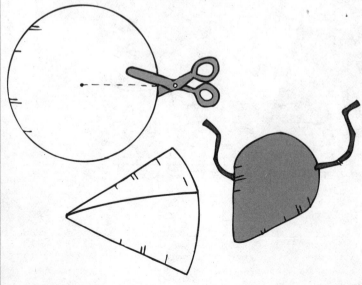

Directions for Making Bills

1. Cut a paper plate from the center to edge. Overlap a quarter of
   the plate to form a cone. Staple
   as illustrated.

2. Punch holes in either side of cone
   and tie yarn through the holes.
   Use yarn ties to secure the bill to
   the child's face. Paint bills black
   or orange.

Two-Bean Meals

Beans are inexpensive and often served in many parts of the world. In Europe, bean soup is sometimes called Poor Man's Soup or Monk's Soup. In Mexico and Central America, beans are usually eaten daily and often take the place of meat.

Two-Bean Soup
Greece

1. Soak beans overnight in plenty of cold water. You will need 1 cup (240 ml) of white beans and 1 cup (240 ml) of kidney beans for each 8 servings of soup.
2. The next day, drain beans and rinse well. Place beans in a large pot with 12 cups (3L) cold water and bring to a boil.
3. Cook 1 hour or until beans are tender.
4. Add 1 chopped onion, 2 large chopped carrots, 1/2 cup (120 ml) tomato paste, 2/3 cup (160 ml) olive oil, 2 tablespoons (30 ml) chopped parsley. Continue cooking until vegetables are tender. Serve hot. Can be seasoned with vinegar, salt and pepper, or garnished with chopped parsley.

Twice-Cooked Beans
Mexico

In Mexico, already-cooked beans are fried. Refried beans are called frijoles. This recipe is easy to use in the classroom. Bring cooked beans to class. You will need 1/4 cup (60 ml) of beans per serving.

1. Using a potato masher, mash the beans and mix well.
2. Using plastic, serrated knives, have children chop green onions and mince garlic cloves. You will need 1 tablespoon (15 ml) of onions and a minced garlic clove for each 2 cups (480 ml) of beans that you are frying. Add the chopped onion and garlic to the cooked beans. You can also add 1 tablespoon (15 ml) of chili powder per cup of beans. If available in your area, chopped fresh cilantro is another tasty addition. Mix thoroughly.
3. Heat 1 to 2 tablespoons (15 to 30 ml) oil in frying pan set at 375°F (191°C). Drop beans by spoonfuls into skillet and fry for 2 minutes on each side or until warm all the way through and slightly crispy on the outside. Serve with warm tortillas or corn bread.

Super!

_____

knows the shape of the number **2**.

Sensational!

You understand the concept of **two**.

To: _____

I'm **so** proud of your work matching pairs!

To: _____

Good for You,

_____!

You memorized two blackbird rhymes!

3 three

I saw three ships come sailing by,
Sailing by, sailing by,
I saw three ships come sailing by,
On New Year's Day in the morning.

And what do you think was in them then,
Was in them then, was in them then,
And what do you think was in them then,
On New Year's Day in the morning?

Three pretty girls were in them then,
Were in them then, were in them then,
Three pretty girls were in them then,
On New Year's Day in the morning.

And one could whistle, and one could sing
And one could play on the violin,
Such joy there was at my wedding,
On New Year's Day in the morning.

Three little kittens they lost their mittens,
And they began to cry,
"Oh! Mammy dear,
We sadly fear,
Our mittens we have lost!"
"What! Lost your mittens,
You naughty kittens,
Then you shall have no pie."
Miew, miew, miew, miew,
Miew, miew, miew, miew.

3 three

Three young rats with black felt hats,
Three young ducks with white straw flats,
Three young dogs with curling tails,
Three young cats with demi-veils;
Went out to walk with three young pigs
In satin vests and sorrel wigs.
But suddenly it chanced to rain
And so they all went home again.

Three blind mice,
See how they run!
They all ran after the farmer's wife,
Who cut off their tails with a carving knife;
Did you ever hear such a thing in your life
As three blind mice?

Rub a dub, dub,
Three men in a tub;
And who do you think they be?
The butcher, the baker,
The candlestick maker
Toss them out–all three!

Blind Mice Trio

Three blind mice,
See how they run!
They all ran after the farmer's wife,
Who cut off their tails with a carving knife;
Did you ever hear such a thing in your life
As three blind mice?

Count to three. Show the students three fingers. Count each finger. Have them show you three fingers and count each one. Then practice singing "Three Blind Mice." When the children know the words, try singing the song as a trio with solo parts. Explain that a trio is sung by three people and a solo is when one person sings alone. Pick a trio to sing the first, second and last lines. Assign individuals to sing lines three, four and five. Break into small groups and let the students organize themselves and sing the rhyme in trio. Give everyone the opportunity to be part of a trio and an opportunity to sing solo.

Three blind mice,	Trio
See how they run!	Trio
They all ran after the farmer's wife,	Solo 1
Who cut off their tails with a carving knife;	Solo 2
Did you ever hear such a thing in your life	Solo 3
As three blind mice?	Trio

Three Men in a Tub

Rub a dub, dub,
Three men in a tub;
And who do you think they be?
The butcher, the baker,
The candlestick maker
Toss them out–all three!

To make a tub of men you will need a plastic berry
basket or small margarine tub for each student.
Reproduce the tub, butcher, baker and candlestick
maker below and on the following page. Children
cut out paper men and color each one. Color and
cut out the front and back of the tub. Glue the verse
to the front of the tub. Glue the back of the tub to the inside of the back of the
berry basket so that the sail shows. Place the men in the tub.

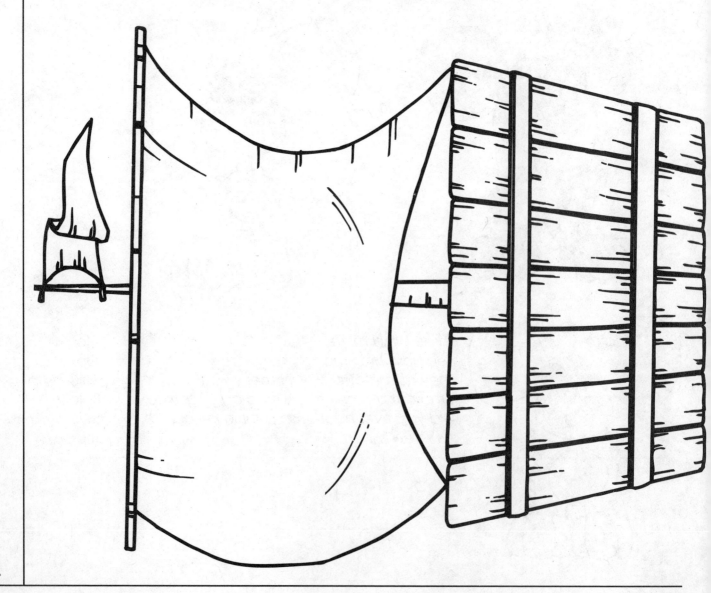

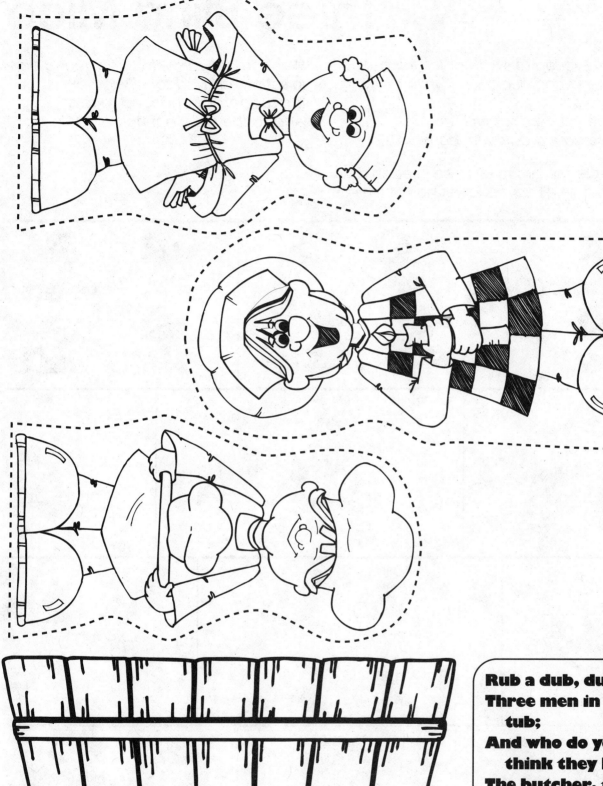

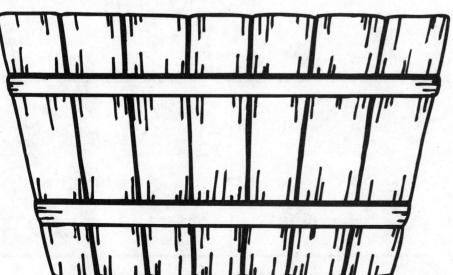

Rub a dub, dub,
Three men in a
   tub;
And who do you
   think they be?
The butcher, the
   baker,
The candlestick
   maker
Toss them out—all
   three!

Three Blind Mice

Three young rats with black felt hats,
Three young ducks with white straw
    flats,
Three young dogs with curling tails,
Three young cats with demi-veils*;

Went out to walk with three young pigs
In satin vests and sorrel wigs.
But suddenly it chanced to rain
And so they all went home again.

Circle the group of three in each row.
*A demi-veil covers lower half of face.

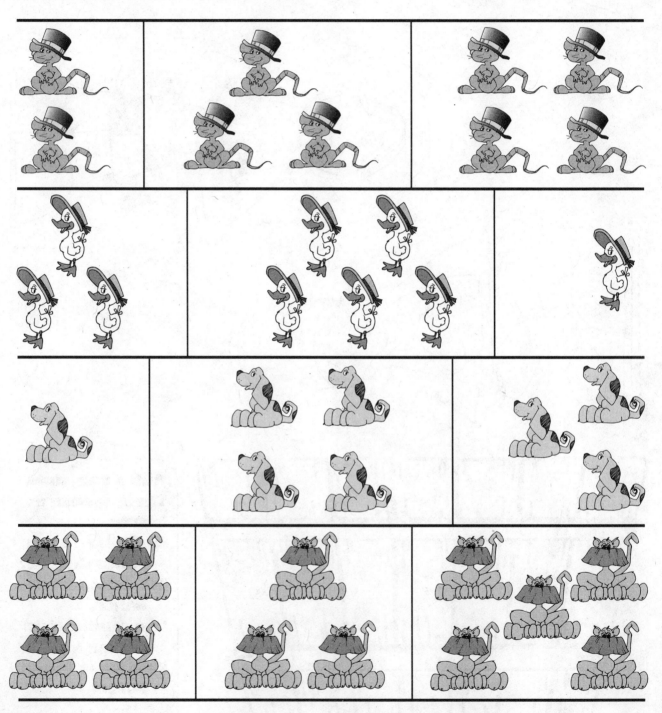

Rub a Dub, Dub, It Floats!

Rub a dub, dub,
Three men in a tub;
And who do you think they be?
The butcher, the baker,
The candlestick maker
Toss them out–all three!

Getting Ready: Place a small wading pool or large tub of water in the center. Collect objects that float and objects that do not float. Place them in a box near the water. Reproduce worksheet below. Change objects in center often.

Objective: After experimenting with objects to see if they sink or float, students are to draw the object on or below the water on the worksheet.

I Saw Three Ships

I saw three ships come sailing by,
Sailing by, sailing by,
I saw three ships come sailing by,
On New Year's Day in the morning.

To discover the mystery picture, color spaces with three dots red. Color spaces with two dots blue.

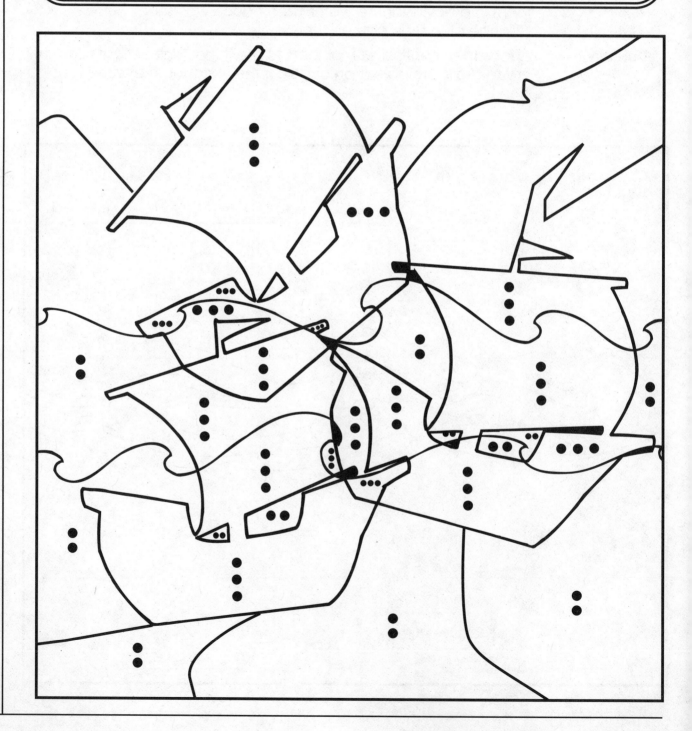

Watch the Bouncing Balls

Cut out the three seals. Matching number words and numerals, paste each seal in the correct place on the next page. Color the picture.

Watch the Bouncing Balls

Use the seals on
the previous page
to complete this page.

one

two

three

A Sea of Threes

I saw three ships come sailing by,
Sailing by, sailing by,
I saw three ships come sailing by,
On New Year's Day in the morning.

Writing the numeral three will be fun when students use blue pudding paint. To make an edible finger paint, you will need instant vanilla pudding, milk, mixing bowl, spoon and blue food coloring. Mix the instant pudding as directed on the back of the package. Stir in a few drops of blue food coloring. Chill until set. Store in refrigerator in a closed container until ready. Use the pudding paint the way you would use any other finger paint. Have children scrub their hands and cover their work area with newspapers before they begin painting. Give each student a large sheet of finger painting paper and a small paper cup of pudding. Encourage students to use the pudding to make an ocean with three sailing ships. Show them how to use the numeral three as birds in the sky.

Writing Idea

Three Blind Mice

Three blind mice,
See how they run!
They all ran after the farmer's wife,
Who cut off their tails with a carving knife;
Did you ever hear such a thing in your life
As three blind mice?

Getting Ready: Three Blind Mice is a tag game. It is best if the children have memorized the rhyme. Each child needs a handkerchief or piece of cloth as used in tag football to tuck in a back pocket (mouse's tail).

Directions: Someone is chosen to be the "farmer" or "farmer's wife." "Farmer's wife" sings the rhyme and then tries to catch and remove the "tails" from as many mice as possible in three minutes. That is her score. Then a new "farmer's wife" is chosen, and the tag game is repeated. Let everyone have the opportunity to be the "farmer's wife" and record her score. The players with the most points at the end of the game are declared the winners.

Variation: After the children have played the game running away from each other, try replacing the word *ran* in the rhyme with *walks, hops* or *skips*. Children chant and move in the appropriate way while being chased by the "farmer's wife."

Three Little Kittens

Recite the whole rhyme to the children. Then turn the rhyme into a short play. Ask for volunteers to play each part. A child who knows all the words to the rhyme should play Mother Cat. The three little kittens should also know the rhyme quite well. Teacher or another student can be the narrator. After practicing the play, let the children perform it for another group of children. Faces painted like cats will add to the performance. Simply use a washable, black marker or eyeliner pencil to draw triangular noses and whiskers on each little kitten and Mother Cat.

Narrator: *Three little kittens they lost their mittens,*
And they began to cry.

Three Kittens: *"Oh! Mammy dear,*
We sadly fear,
Our mittens we have lost!"

Mother Cat: *"What! Lost your mittens,*
You naughty kittens,
Then you shall have no pie."

Chorus: *Miew, miew, miew, miew,*
Miew, miew, miew, miew.

Narrator: *The three little kittens they found their mittens,*
And they began to cry.

Three Kittens: *"Oh! Mammy dear,*
See here, see here,
Our mittens we have found."

Mother Cat: *"What! Found your mittens,*
You darling kittens,
Then you shall have some pie."

Chorus: *Purr, purr, purr, purr,*
Purr, purr, purr, purr.

Narrator: *The three little kittens put on their mittens,*
And soon ate up the pie.

Three Kittens: *"Oh! Mammy dear,*
We greatly fear,
Our mittens we have soiled."

Dramatic Play

Dramatic Play

Mother Cat: *"What! Soiled your mittens,*
You naughty kittens!"

Narrator: *Then they began to sigh.*

Chorus: *Miew, miew, miew, miew,*
Miew, miew, miew, miew.

Narrator: *The three little kittens they washed their mittens,*
And hung them up to dry.

Three Kittens: *"Oh! Mammy dear,*
Look here, look here,
Our mittens we have washed."

Mother Cat: *"What! Washed your mittens,*
You darling kittens!
But I smell a rat close by!
Hush! Hush!"

Chorus: *Miew, miew, miew, miew,*
Miew, miew, miew, miew.

Three Ways to Cook Pears

A pie sat on a pear tree,
A pie sat on a pear tree,
A pie sat on a pear tree,
Heigh O, heigh O, heigh O!

Pear Jam
Sweden

1. Wash, peel, core and chop 2 pounds (.9 kg) ripe pears.
2. In a large saucepan, combine 2 cups (280 ml) peeled, cored and chopped pears; 2 cups (480 ml) water; juice of 1 lemon and a $1^3/4$-ounce (49.61 g) package powdered fruit pectin.
3. Stir over high heat until mixture boils hard. Stir in 4 cups (960 ml) sugar and bring to a full rolling boil; boil hard 1 minute stirring constantly. Remove from heat.
4. Pour into hot sterilized jelly glasses. Seal at once. When cool, refrigerate until using. Makes six jars of jelly.

Pear Sauce
Israel

1. Wash 8-10 pears. Coarsely chop.
2. Place pears, juice from 1 lemon and 1 thin strip lemon rind in a slow cooker. Add 4 tablespoons (60 ml) sugar and $1/4$ cup (60 ml) water. Cover and cook on high about an hour until pears are a pulp.
3. Rub through a sieve or mash until smooth. Add 1 tablespoon (15 ml) butter. Beat well. Cool and chill. To make pear butter, cook pears another hour or until they are as thick as jam. Cool and chill.

Fresh Pear Pie
United States

1. Place one ready-made pie crust in a glass pie dish. Bake crust for 15 minutes at 375°F (191°C) or until golden. Remove from oven and cool.
2. Wash, peel, core and chop 2 pounds (.9 kg) ripe pears. Mix with 2 cups (480 ml) vanilla pudding or 2 cups (480 ml) whipped cream. Chill.
3. Place pears in cooled baked shell. Sprinkle with 1 tablespoon (15 ml) cinnamon and 2 tablespoons (30 ml) sugar.

Beautiful Work!

_____

knows the shape of the number **3**.

Blue Ribbon for You

You understand the concept of **three**.

To: _____

Top Banana!

Good work, singing trio!

To: _____

Good for You, _____!

You were very good in the "Three Little Kittens" play.

4 four

One for the money,
Two for the show,
Three to make ready,
And four to go.

Here we go 'round the mulberry bush,
The mulberry bush, the mulberry bush,
Here we go 'round the mulberry bush,
On a cold and frosty morning.

I had four brothers over the sea.
Perrie, Merrie, Dixie, Dominie.
And they each sent a present unto me,
Petrum, Partrum, Paradise, Temporie,
Perrie, Merrie, Dixie, Dominie.

I Had Four Brothers

Circle Time

Read all the verses of the rhyme below to the children. Before reading the last two verses, give them time to solve each riddle. (The last verses are the answers to the riddles.) Put each riddle in simple terms and lead them to the answers by asking questions. Examples: How can a chicken have no bones? How can a cherry have no stone?

I had four brothers over the sea.
Perrie, Merrie, Dixie, Dominie.
And they each sent a present unto me,
Petrum, Partrum, Paradise, Temporie,
Perrie, Merrie, Dixie, Dominie.

The first sent a chicken, without any bones;
The second sent a cherry, without any stones,
Petrum, Partrum, Paradise, Temporie,
Perrie, Merrie, Dixie, Dominie.

The third sent a book which cannot be read;
The fourth sent a blanket, without any thread.
Petrum, Partrum, Paradise, Temporie,
Perrie, Merrie, Dixie, Dominie.

How could there be a chicken without any bones?
How could there be a cherry without any stones?
Petrum, Partrum, Paradise, Temporie,
Perrie, Merrie, Dixie, Dominie.

How could there be a book which cannot be read?
How could there be a blanket, without a thread?

Answers:
When the chicken's in the eggshell, there are no bones,
When the cherry's in the blossom, there are no stones.
Petrum, Partrum, Paradise, Temporie,
Perrie, Merrie, Dixie, Dominie.

When the book's in the press, it cannot be read;
When the wool's on the sheep's back,
  there is no thread.
Petrum, Partrum, Paradise, Temporie,
Perrie, Merrie, Dixie, Dominie.

Four Brothers over the Sea

I had four brothers over the sea.
Perrie, Merrie, Dixie, Dominie.
And they each sent a present unto me,
Petrum, Partrum, Paradise, Temporie,
Perrie, Merrie, Dixie, Dominie.

To make four floating paper brothers,
you will need a bar of Ivory™ soap,
toothpicks and the patterns for each
student. Reproduce patterns of the
four brothers on the following page
on heavy paper or light cardboard.
Give a set of four men to each stu-
dent. Cut out and color the paper men with crayons, markers or paint. Place
each man on the sticky side of a sheet of clear adhesive paper. Put a toothpick
at the base of each man as illustrated and press in place. Cover with another
piece of clear adhesive paper and press to seal. Carefully trim around edges as
illustrated. To make the men stand on their boat, poke one end of each toothpick
into the top of the bar of soap.

Variation: Let children race their boats in a small wading pool or large tub of
water. Later the boats can be taken home and used in the bathtub.

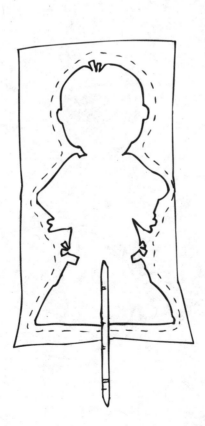

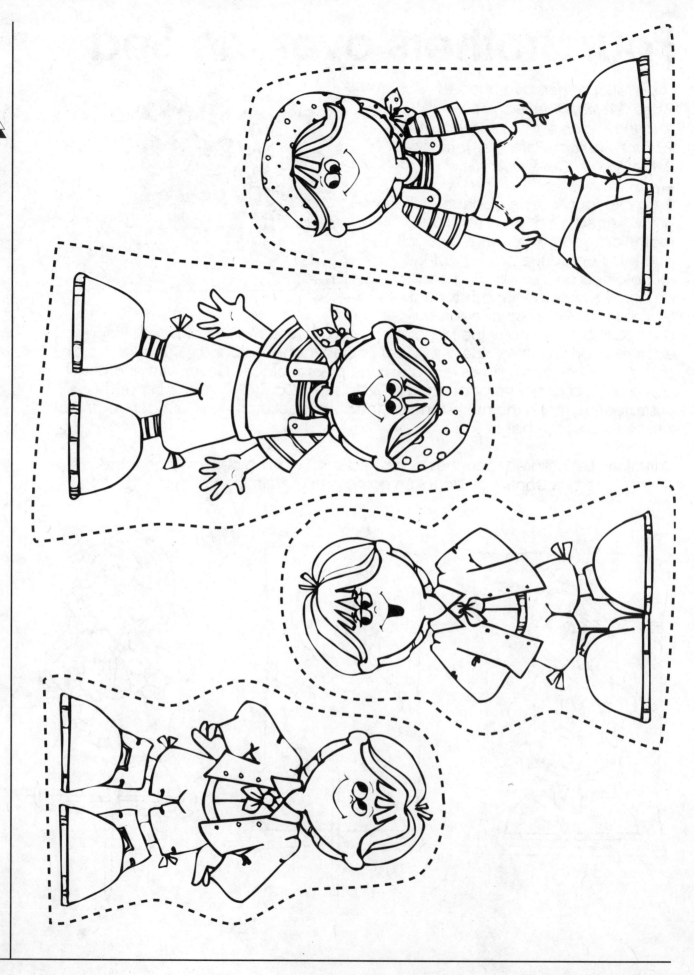

Four Presents

I had four brothers over the sea.
Perrie, Merrie, Dixie, Dominie.
And they each sent a present unto me,
Petrum, Partrum, Paradise, Temporie,
Perrie, Merrie, Dixie, Dominie.

Match the number four to the set of four. Draw a line from the numeral to the correct picture.

4

Show Business

One for the money,
Two for the show,
Three to make ready,
And four to go.

Getting Ready: You can stimulate imaginative play with a dress-up center. Gather old party dresses, men's suits, assorted hats, jackets, oversized shoes and other interesting clothes. Wash them in the washing machine. Place on hangers and hang in the dress-up center. Also place a full-length mirror, occupational props (fire fighter's hat, police officer's badge, etc.) and an egg timer in the center.

Objective: Students are to choose an outfit and get dressed in just four minutes. Then they can play in the clothes as long as they wish. Set the timer for four minutes when removing and hanging up clothes, too.

Four to Match!

Circle the set of four children in this picture. Color the picture.

"Din-a-Four"

Reproduce the "din-a-four" on heavy paper or light cardboard. Cut out. Matching the number words and the numerals, cut out and paste the scales on the din-a-four's back. Color each of the four scales a different color.

Floating Fours

One for the money,
Two for the show,
Three to make ready,
And four to go.

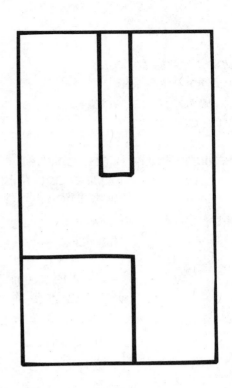

If the sculptor is trying to form round or intricate shapes, carving soap isn't easy. But a basic square shape is a good first project when learning to carve soap. Give each child a square bar of soft soap such as Ivory™. Mark each bar of soap indicating what should be carved out as illustrated. (Save all of the shavings for soap paint. See recipe on page 112.) After all the fours are carved, talk about how they look from the side, from the back, looking down on them from the top or looking up from the bottom. Children can take home the fours and float them in their bath.

Writing Idea ◇

Four to Go!

One for the money,
Two for the show,
Three to make ready,
And four to go!

Getting Ready: Many children enjoy racing. Choose an open area where a starting line and finishing line can be drawn or designated and divide class into groups of four.

Directions: Have four children race at one time. The winner of each race should receive an award. (See awards below and on pages 75 and 76.) Use the rhyme to have the children who are not racing signal the beginning of each race. To add variety and fun to racing and give students who do not run very fast a chance to win, try some of the following:

Rabbit race–Have regular running races.

Snail race–Use arms and legs and move along on stomach.

Flamingo race–Hop on one foot.

Turtle race–Move on hands and knees.

Kangaroo race–Hop with both feet together.

Spider race–Move along on fingertips and tiptoes.

Spry as a Spider Award!

To: _____

From: _____

Date: _____

_____
Signature

You Are as Quick as a Rabbit!

To: _____

From: _____

Date: _____

_____
Signature

Snail Crawl Award!

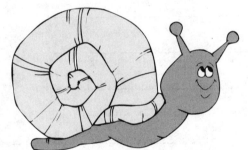

To: _____

From: _____

Date: _____

_____
Signature

Snake Slithering Award!

To: _____

From: _____

Date: _____

_____
Signature

Flamingo Flingo Award!

To: _____

From: _____

Date: _____

_____
Signature

Turtle Racing Award!

To: _____

From: _____

Date: _____

_____
Signature

Kangaroo Hopping Award!

To: _____

From: _____

Date: _____

_____
Signature

The Turtle Race

One for the money,
Two for the show,
Three to make ready,
And four to go.

Getting Ready: Reproduce pages 78 and 79. If you want more than one game-board, reproduce each page several times. Attach the game-board halves to the inside of a file folder. Color the board. Cover with clear adhesive paper. Paste the game rules on the cover of the file folder. If you wish, cover the front of the folder with clear adhesive paper, too.

The Turtle Race

This game is for 2 to 3 players.

Materials:
one game marker for each player
one coin

Rules:
1. Place game markers in the "Go" space.
2. Flip the coin to see who goes first. Heads win. If more than one person flips heads, flip again.
3. Flip the coin. Heads move ahead 2 spaces. Tails move ahead 1 space. Name the number you land on. If you can name it, you stay. If you cannot name it, you move back 1 space.
4. Pass coin to the next player.
5. Continue playing until one player crosses the finish line.

File Folder Game

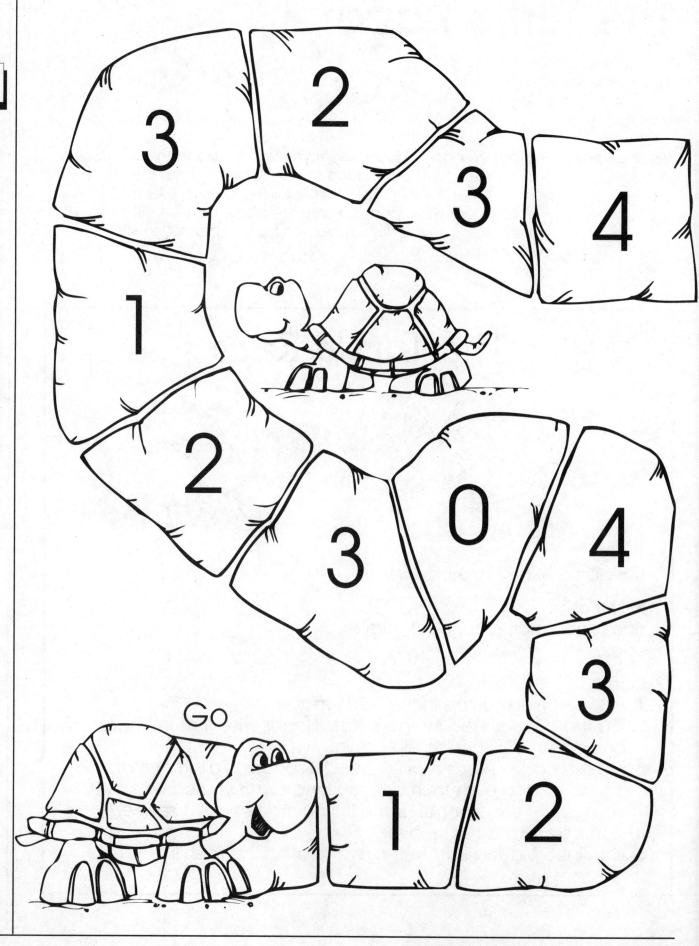

Go

Finish

Here We Go 'Round the Mulberry Bush

Recite the rhyme one verse at a time. Ask the children to count how many times they hear key words (verse 1: mulberry bush, verse 2: wash our hands, verse 3: wash our clothes, verse 4: go to school, verse 5: come out of school). Then break into five groups. Give each group a different verse. (See enlarged verses below and on the next page.) Each group is to work out actions for its verse and practice them. Meeting again as a large group, recite the rhyme. Have each group demonstrate its movements and teach them to the rest of the class. Then say the whole rhyme as everyone uses appropriate actions.

Here we go 'round the mulberry bush,
The mulberry bush, the mulberry bush,
Here we go 'round the mulberry bush,
On a cold and frosty morning.

This is the way we wash our hands,
Wash our hands, wash our hands,
This is the way we wash our hands,
On a cold and frosty morning.

This is the way we wash our clothes,
Wash our clothes, wash our clothes,
This is the way we wash our clothes,
On a cold and frosty morning.

This is the way we go to school,
Go to school, go to school,
This is the way we go to school,
On a cold and frosty morning.

This is the way we leave our school,
Leave our school, leave our school,
This is the way we leave our school,
On a cold and frosty morning.

Four Ways to Cook Carrots

Carrot Cake
Germany

1. Preheat oven to 350°F (177°C). Generously butter the bottom and sides of a cake pan. Flour the pan.
2. Let the children scrape and then grate 4 large carrots per cake.
3. Cream $1/2$ cup (120 ml) butter and $1/2$ cup (120 ml) brown sugar. Add 2 eggs and mix well.
4. Stir in 1 cup (240 ml) flour, 1 teaspoon (5 ml) baking powder and $1/2$ teaspoon (2.5 ml) baking soda. Mix thoroughly.
5. Add 2 tablespoons (30 ml) milk. Stir.
6. Add carrots and 1 cup (240 ml) chopped nuts. Stir by hand until well blended.
7. Pour into pan and bake 30-45 minutes or until a knife inserted into the cake comes out clean.
8. When cool, cake can be iced with cream cheese frosting.

Carrot and Pineapple Pudding
Mexico

1. Cook 1 pound (.45 kg) of scraped and chopped carrots until soft. Mash.
2. Peel and chop the fruit of one large pineapple. If a fresh pineapple is not available, canned may be used, but drain the pineapple pieces thoroughly. Chop the pineapple into small pieces and mix with the carrots.
3. Add $1/2$ cup (120 ml) sugar to carrot mixture and put into a saucepan. Cook over low heat for about 15 minutes, stirring constantly.
4. Beat 2 egg yolks until fluffy. Stir a little of the hot carrot mixture into the eggs, then stir back into the pan. Continue cooking for 5 more minutes. Stir constantly.
5. Turn into a flat dish or pan and spread to about 1" to 2" (2.54 to 5.08 cm) thick. Chill. When set, cut into diamond shapes. Keep cold until serving. Mixture is rather like a soft candy or fudge.

Four Ways to Cook Carrots

Carrots Flemish

Belgium

1. Wash 1 pound (.45 kg) carrots and cut into chunks.
2. Boil carrots in salted water for 5 minutes. Drain well.
3. Melt 1/4 cup (60 ml) butter in a pan, add the carrots and just enough boiling water to cover. Add salt, pepper and 1/2 teaspoon (2.5 ml) sugar. Cook the carrots until they are very tender.
4. Lightly beat 1 egg yolk with 2 tablespoons (30 ml) cream and add to carrots. Hold the pan just off the heat to finish cooking.

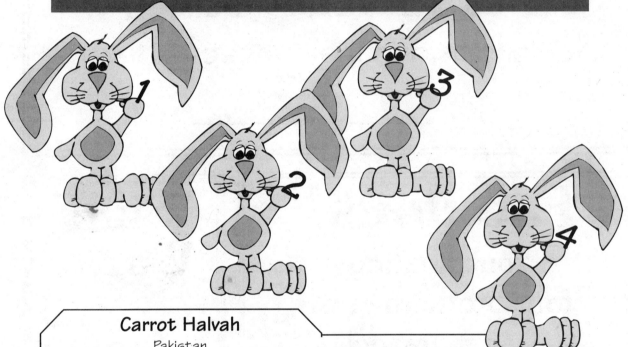

Carrot Halvah

Pakistan

1. Scrape 1 pound (.45 kg) of carrots and shred them into long strips. It is very important that the carrot shreds be as long as possible.
2. Bring 1 quart (.95 l) of milk to a boil in a large pan. Add the carrots and cook over a simmering heat until the carrots are thick and soft and all the milk has been absorbed, between 2 and 3 hours. Can be done in a slow cooker. Stir from time to time.
3. Add 3/4 cup (180 ml) sugar and 2 tablespoons (30 ml) butter.
4. Stir well and pour this mixture into another hot but dry pan and boil, stirring constantly until the mixture begins to solidify and change to a deep red color. Can be served both hot or cold.

Fine!

_____

knows the shape of the number **4**.

Fantastic!

You understand the concept of **four**.

To: _____

Fabulous!

**Your floating
four brothers craft
was fantastic!**

To: _____

Fine
Work,

_____ **!**

I'm very fond of all
the fine work you
have finished with
the number four.

TLC10011 Copyright © Teaching & Learning Company, Carthage, IL 62321

5 five

This little pig went to market.
This little pig stayed home.
This little pig had roast beef.
This little pig had none.
This little pig cried wee, wee, wee
all the way home.

Here comes a poor woman from baby
land,
With five small children on her hand:
One can brew, the other can bake,
The other can make a pretty round
cake,
One can sit in the garden and spin,
Another can make a fine bed for the
king:
Pray, madam, will you take one in?

One, two, three, four,
five,
Catching fishes all alive.
Why did you let them
go?
Because they bit my
finger so.
Which finger did they
bite?
The little finger on the
right.

Elizabeth, Elspeth, Betsy and Bess,
They all went together to seek a bird's
nest.
They found a bird's nest with five eggs in,
They all took one and left four in.

Little Finger on the Right

One, two, three, four, five,
Catching fishes all alive.
Why did you let them go?
Because they bit my finger so.
Which finger did they bite?
The little finger on the right.

Count to five. Show the children five fingers. Count each finger. Have the children count their fingers. Recite the rhyme and show the appropriate number of fingers for each word of the first line. As you recite the rhyme, encourage children to perform the appropriate actions. When the class has memorized the rhyme, let the boys ask the questions and girls answer, or vice versa. Distinguish the left and right hand for reciting the last line of rhyme.

Variation: Have students remove their shoes and count their toes on each foot. Use toes for reciting the "This Little Pig Went to Market" rhyme.

This little pig went to market.
This little pig stayed home.
This little pig had roast beef.
This little pig had none.
This little pig cried wee, wee, wee all the way home.

This Little Pig Plaque

This little pig went to market.
This little pig stayed home.
This little pig had roast beef.
This little pig had none.
This little pig cried wee, wee, wee all the way home.

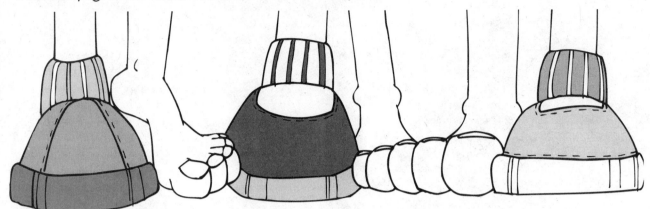

To make footprint plaques, you will need poster paint, heavy 12" (30.48 cm) paper plates, hole punch, yarn, a cake pan as long and as wide as a child's foot and a sponge cut to fit in the bottom of cake pan. Wet the sponge and wring out excess water. Place the damp sponge in the cake pan and pour a little paint on it. There should be just enough paint to make the sponge damp but not soggy. Have a pan of hot sudsy water and a towel ready for cleanup. Ask students to remove one shoe. Place one foot on the sponge, lift foot out of pan and step in the center of a paper plate. Next, place foot in tub of water for cleanup. When paint dries, children can use the hole punch to put evenly spaced holes around the edge of plate. Weave yarn around the edges of the plate. Attach a yarn loop for a hanger. Glue a copy of the box below on the back of each plate. Write the student's name and date on the back of each plaque, too.

This little pig went to market.
This little pig stayed home.
This little pig had roast beef.
This little pig had none.
This little pig cried wee, wee, wee
  all the way home.

Name: _____

Date: _____

Five Fine Fish

Number Recognition

Circle the groups of five.

Five-Day Paint Center

This little pig went to market.
This little pig stayed home.
This little pig had roast beef.
This little pig had none.
This little pig cried wee, wee, wee all the way home.

Getting Ready: A painting center where children can use paints at their leisure is a good way to stimulate creative expression. Place a drop cloth under several easels. Put paint in plastic jars with lids. It is most convenient if the painting center is near a sink with water for easy cleanup. Each day for five days, place a different line of the rhyme in the center. (See reproducible enlarged rhyme on the following page.)

Objective: Children paint a picture of each day's line. After paint dries, encourage children to write a word, or you can print the day's line at the bottom of each painting. When all the pictures are finished, staple each child's work together to create a book.

Variation: You may choose to set up a painting table instead of easels. Cover table with an oil cloth or newspapers. Put paper and paints at the table. In addition to brushes, make available cotton swabs, sponges, sticks, corks, feathers, string and other objects for spreading paint. Encourage students to use their fingers and hands to spread paint, too.

TLC10011 Copyright © Teaching & Learning Company, Carthage, IL 62321

This little pig went to market.

This little pig stayed home.

This little pig had roast beef.

This little pig had none.

This little pig cried wee, wee, wee all the way home.

Finding Little Pigs

This little pig went to market.
This little pig stayed home.
This little pig had roast beef.

This little pig had none.
This little pig cried wee, wee, wee all the way home.

Hidden in the picture are all five little pigs. Can you find them? Circle the pigs and color the picture.

This Little Pig Went to Market

Help the five little pigs get to market. There are different paths through the maze. Find and color each of the paths a different color.

Market

Five Live Fish

One, two, three, four, five,
Catching fishes all alive.
Why did you let them go?
Because they bit my finger so.
Which finger did they bite?
The little finger on the right.

Directions: Can you catch five fish?
Color each one. Cut out the fish.
Glue a paper clip to the back of
each fish. Use a magnet to pick up
the fish in order from 1-5.
Challenge: Tie the magnet onto the
end of a piece of string.

Cut and Paste

All Took One

Elizabeth, Elspeth, Betsy and Bess,
They all went together to seek a bird's nest.
They found a bird's nest with five eggs in,
They all took one and left four in.

How could four girls each take an egg and leave four eggs in the nest? Answer: There is just one girl. The last three names are all nicknames for Elizabeth. Help children use their name and three nicknames to rewrite the rhyme. Fill in the four blanks in the poem for each student. Then have the children draw and color a picture.

_____, _____, _____ and _____,

They all went together to seek a bird's nest.

They found a bird's nest with 5 eggs in,

They all took 1 and left 4 in. How can that be?

Jump Rope Rhymes

One, two, three, four, five,
Catching fishes all alive.
Why did you let them go?
Because they bit my finger so.
Which finger did they bite?
The little finger on the right.

Getting Ready: Many preschoolers cannot jump rope. Begin teaching children how to jump rope by having them jump to the rhythm of a rhyme, each turning his own imaginary rope. Demonstrate how to jump while pretending to swing a rope over your head and then under your feet at the appropriate time.

Directions: Use ropes and try jumping five times on each line of the rhyme. (Jump on each underlined word or word pair.)

One, two, three, four, five,
Catching fishes all a/live.
Why did you let them go?
Because they bit my finger so.
Which finger did they bite?
The little finger on the right.

Variation: Later, after students have had plenty of time to practice this rhyme, use some of the other rhymes for five as jump rope rhymes. See the suggestions on the following page.

Game

Jump Rope Rhymes

Jump on each word or cluster of words as indicated.

　　　Here comes/a poor/woman/from/baby land,

　　　With five/small/children/on/her hand:

　　　One can/brew,/the other/can bake,

　　　The other/can make/a pretty/round cake,

　　　One can/sit/in the garden/and spin,

　　　Another/can make/a fine bed/for the king:

　　　Pray,/madam,/will you/take/one in?

Variation: Hot Peppers rope jumping means to pull the rope under the feet twice on one jump. Use this rhyme for practicing jumping hot peppers. Pull the rope under the feet two times for each group of words. Only a few will master using a rope to jump this fast.

　　　Elizabeth,/Elspeth,/Betsy/and Bess,

　　　They all/went together/to seek/a bird's/nest.

　　　They found/a bird's nest/with five/eggs/in,

　　　They all/took/one/and left/four/in.

Discussion: Explain syncopation to the children. In syncopation, the off beats are stressed. When you walk, your feet make a regular beat. When you skip, your feet make a syncopated rhythm. Jumping rope makes regular rhythms, while Double Dutch rope jumping is an example of syncopation. For a real challenge, let the students who want to try it, practice syncopation by jumping Double Dutch to every word of the rhyme below. Two people turn two ropes in opposite directions while a third person jumps both ropes. This will take a great deal of practice. For the few that can jump Double Dutch, let them practice and demonstrate syncopated jumping for the other students.

　　　Little <u>Jack</u>/Dandy-<u>prat</u>/was <u>my</u>/first <u>suitor</u>;

　　　He <u>had</u>/a <u>dish</u>/and a <u>spoon</u>,/and <u>he had</u>/some <u>pewter</u>;

　　　He <u>had</u>/<u>linen</u>/and <u>woolen</u>,/and <u>linen</u>,

　　　A little <u>pig</u>/in a <u>string</u>/cost <u>him</u>/five <u>shilling</u>.

A Clapping Game

Present the rhyme by reading it once to the class. Repeat as a choral reading. Everyone says the first line. Girls say the second, fourth and last lines. Boys say the third and fifth lines. Then play a clapping game. To play, each child will need to sit facing a partner. *Slap* indicates slapping the knees with palm of hands.

One, two, three, four, five,
Catching fishes all alive.

(Slap, clap, slap, clap.)
(Partners clap right hands, clap,
partners clap left hands, clap.)

Why did you let them go?
Because they bit my finger so.

(Slap, clap, slap, clap)
(Partners clap right hands, clap,
partners clap left hands, clap.)

Which finger did they bite?
The little finger on the right.

(Slap, clap, slap, clap.)
(Partners clap right hands, clap,
partners clap left hands, clap.)

Dramatic Play

Five-Favorite-Fruits Salad

Make a list of favorite fruits on the chalkboard where everyone can see it. Allow children a chance to vote for their five favorite fruits. Then tally the votes and find out what are the top five favorite fruits of the children in your class. Ask each child to bring one or two pieces of one of the chosen five favorite fruits to class. When the fruits are gathered, the salad can be created.

Five-Favorite-Fruits Salad

1. Each child can wash and dry a piece of fruit. Peel, remove seeds and chop fruit into bite-sized chunks.
2. Place fruit in a large bowl. Toss to mix.
3. Chill.
4. If desired, top with whipped cream.

Awesome!

_____

knows the shape of the number **5**.

Amazing!

You understand the concept of **five**.

To: _____

All Right!

_____

can count to five!

Perfect Painting!

To: _____

Your five little pigs paintings are wonderful!

Astounding Rope Jumping!

To: _____

Six Is Half of a Dozen

My father he died, but I can't tell you how;
He left me six horses to drive in my plough;
With my wing, wang, waddle O,
Jack sing saddle O,
Blowsey boys bubble O,
Under the broom.

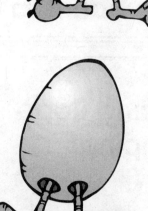

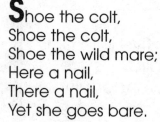

Hickety, pickety, my black hen,
She lays six eggs for gentlemen;
Gentlemen come every day,
To see what my black hen doth lay.

Shoe the colt,
Shoe the colt,
Shoe the wild mare;
Here a nail,
There a nail,
Yet she goes bare.

Six Eggs for Gentlemen

Hickety, pickety, my black hen,
She lays six eggs for gentlemen;
Gentlemen come every day,
To see what my black hen doth lay.

Count to six. Show the children that six are all the fingers on one hand plus one more finger. Show them that six are three fingers on one hand and three fingers on the other hand. Let them experiment to make combinations of fingers that total six. Then draw a row of six eggs on the chalkboard and ask, "Is this six?" Repeat several times. Draw five eggs and ask, "How many more eggs do I need to make six?"

This rhyme can easily be turned into a participation story. Begin by saying the rhyme. When children know the rhyme, have them make the indicated sounds after certain words in the rhyme. A child or group of children can be responsible for saying each of the sounds. Assign parts.

hen	(Cluck, cluck.)
six	(Count to six.)
gentlemen	(How do you do?)
come every day	(Knock six times.)
lay	(Sigh.)

Hickety, pickety, my black hen (Cluck, cluck.),
She lays six (1, 2, 3, 4, 5, 6) *eggs for gentlemen* (How do you do?);
Gentlemen (How do you do?) *come every day* (Knock six times.),
To see what my black hen (cluck, cluck) *doth lay* (Sigh.).

Six Silly Snakes Mobile

To make a mobile with six 6-shaped snakes, you will need six snakes cut using the pattern below and a 6" (15.24 cm) paper plate for each student. Precut snakes. Have each student count his own six snakes. See if anyone notices that the snakes are shaped like the numeral six. Color the snakes' eyes on both sides. Decorate with spots, stripes, diamonds or other geometrical designs. Color with paint, crayons, markers or paper cutouts. Punch a hole in each snake. Punch six evenly spaced holes around the edges of a paper plate. Use various lengths of yarn to attach the snakes to the paper plate as illustrated. Attach a yarn loop in the center of paper plate for hanging mobile.

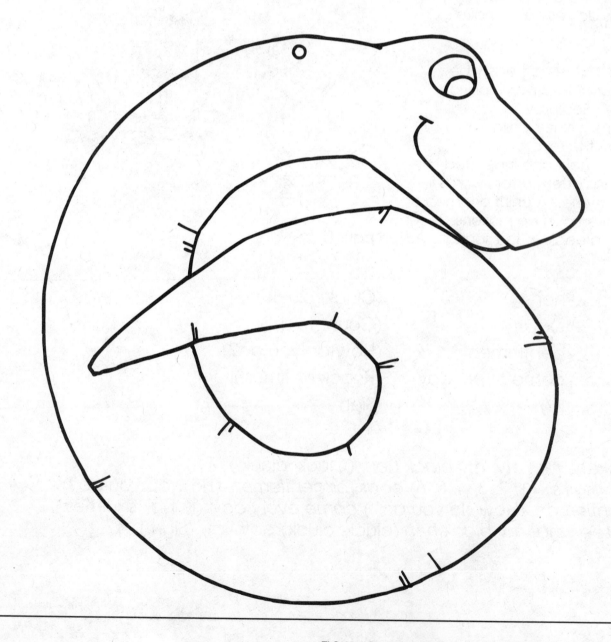

Six Eggs

Which hen has laid six eggs?

Hickety, pickety, my black hen,
She lays six eggs for gentlemen;
Gentlemen come every day,
To see what my black hen doth lay.

Six Eggs Center

Hickety, pickety, my black hen,
She lays six eggs for gentlemen;
Gentlemen come every day,
To see what my black hen doth lay.

Getting Ready: Gather several ½ dozen egg cartons, the ones that hold only six eggs, and an assortment of different colored plastic eggs. Place on a table in learning center. Reproduce task cards below and on pages 105 and 106. Cut apart cards and mount on heavy paper or light cardboard. Place task cards in a box or wire basket at the learning center.

Objective: Children use the egg cartons and plastic eggs to solve the picture problems on the task cards.

Hickety, Pickety Task Cards

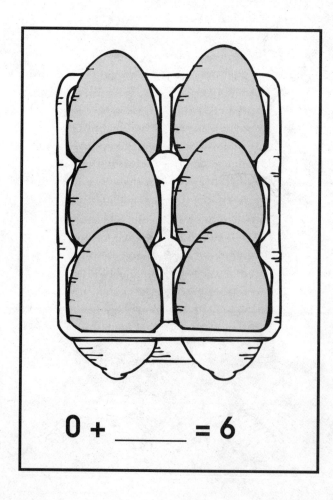

0 + _____ = 6

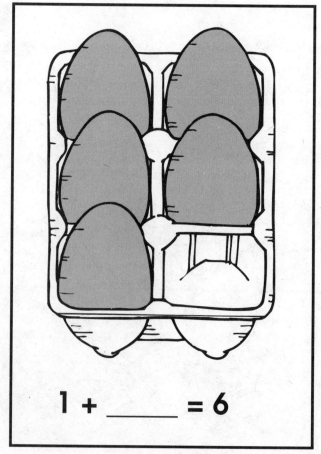

1 + _____ = 6

Learning Center

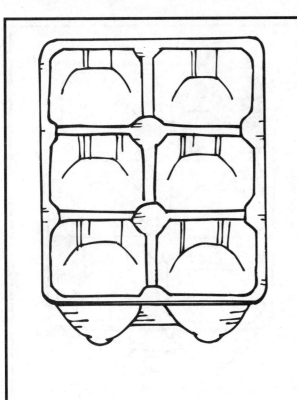

6 + _____ = 6

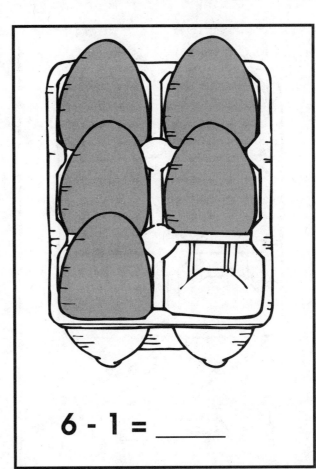

6 - 1 = _____

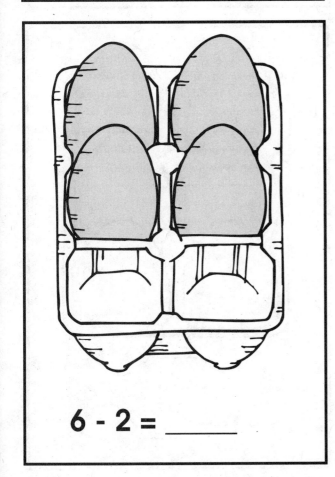

6 - 2 = _____

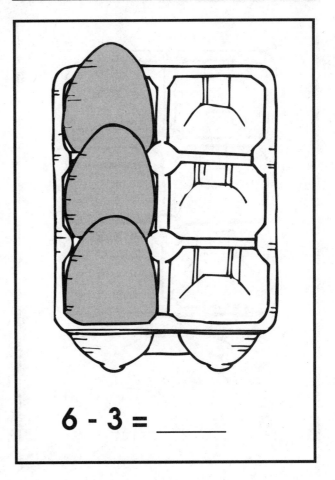

6 - 3 = _____

Learning Center

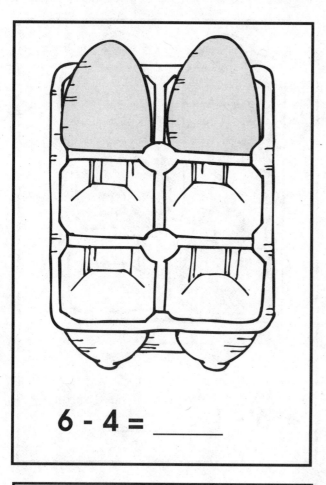

6 - 4 = _____

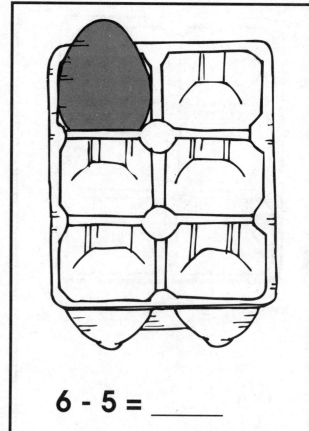

6 - 5 = _____

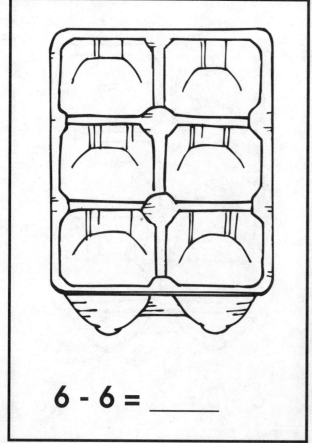

6 - 6 = _____

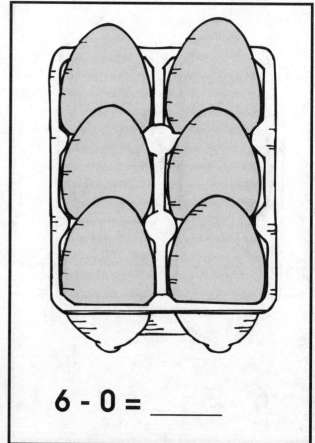

6 - 0 = _____

Eggs in a Nest

Hickety, pickety, my black hen,
She lays six eggs for gentlemen;
Gentlemen come every day,
To see what my black hen doth lay.

Draw six large eggs in the nest. Color each of the eggs a different color. Color the nest yellow or brown. Color the hen black.

Six Hidden Nails

Shoe the colt,
Shoe the colt,
Shoe the wild mare;
Here a nail,
There a nail,
Yet she goes bare.

Hidden in the picture are six horseshoes and six nails. Can you find them? Circle them and color the picture.

Six Ice-Cream Cones

Cut out each scoop of ice cream below. Paste each scoop on the cone with the matching number on page 110.

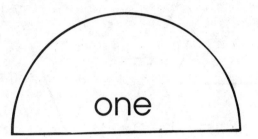

one

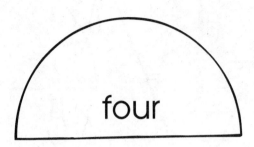

four

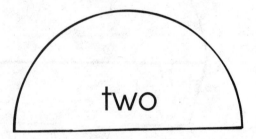

two

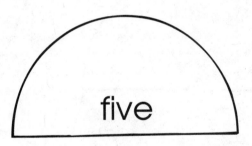

five

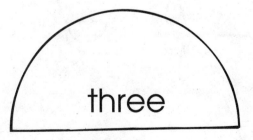

three

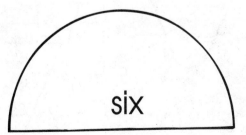

six

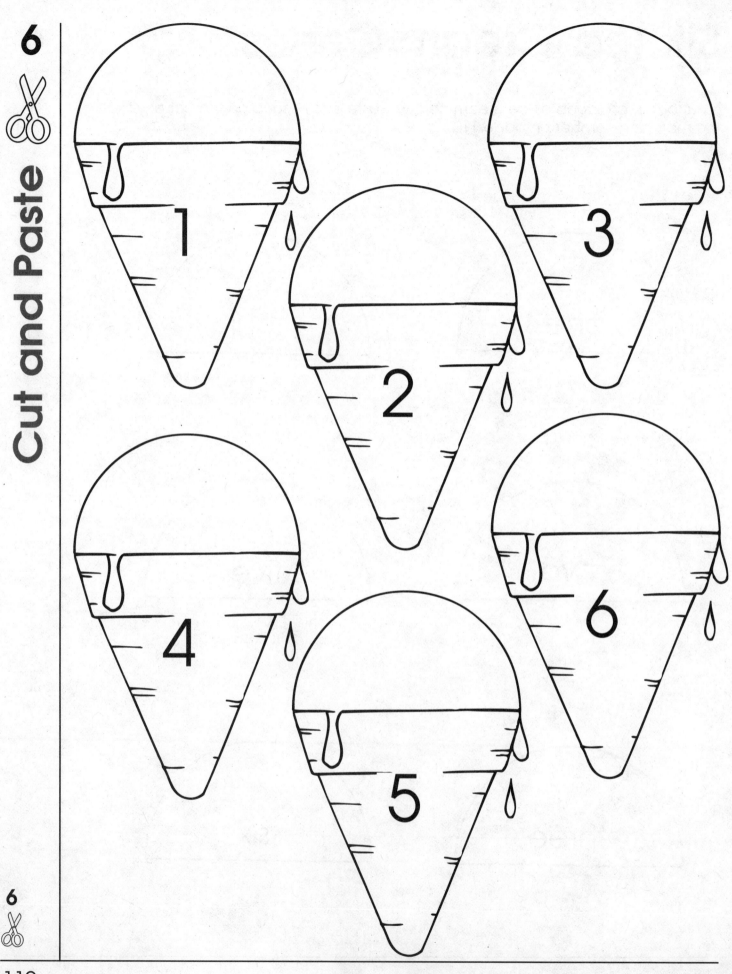

Cut and Paste

Licorice Whip Numbers

Candy usually adds a little motivation for learning. However, if you prefer not to use candy in the classroom, see variation for this activity listed below. To make licorice whip numerals, each child will need a clean, smooth work space. You may want to cover desktops with a sheet of waxed paper. Give each child two thin licorice whips. Demonstrate how to turn a string into the number six. Then have the children try to make a six with their candy. This isn't easy because licorice tends to straighten. Next see what other numerals or shapes the children can make with their licorice whips. Discuss which numeral was the most difficult to make. Which was the easiest? When you are finished, let the children eat their candy.

Variation: Use wet, cooked noodles or spaghetti pasta to form the numerals. Place on paper and let dry. Food coloring can be added to the wet pasta to make a colorful writing medium.

Soapy Sixes

Make and use fluffy soap paint to paint the numeral six. You will need heavy, smooth, white paper; Ivory™ flakes or soap shavings; water; mixing bowl; spoon; electric mixer; food coloring; paintbrushes; newspaper; pencils; a large bowl and six small containers. Boil the soap shavings or Ivory™ flakes in an equal amount of water. Cool. Use a mixer to whip soap mixture in a large bowl until thick and stiff. Put "fluffy" paint in small containers. Add food coloring to make the primary and secondary colors. Mix with a spoon. With a pencil, children lightly draw a large six or several small sixes on their papers. Students can use paintbrushes or fingers to spread the "fluffy" paint on the numerals. Let dry. When dry, trace the outline of the number lightly with fingers.

Follow the Leader

My father he died, but I can't tell you how;
He left me six horses to drive in my plough;
With my wing, wang, waddle O,

Jack sing saddle O,
Blowsey boys bubble O,
Under the broom.

Getting Ready: Before playing Follow the Leader, teach youngsters the rhyme. Because the rhyme is nonsense, it may take awhile to memorize. When children know the rhyme, break into groups of six. Each child in a group holds the waist of the child in front of him to form a line. The first child is the leader. Singing the rhyme six times, the group gallops like horses, and moves in the direction the leader takes them. When the rhyme has been recited six times, the leader moves to the back of the line, and the next person in line is the new leader. Continue reciting the rhyme and moving until every child has had an opportunity to be the leader.

Variation: The leader only recites the first line, substituting another animal for horse and moves in a way that indicates that animal. The other five recite the rest of the rhyme. Example: "He left me six frogs to drive in my plough." Children hop like frogs instead of galloping like horses.

Discussion: What other animals can we name in the rhyme? How do these animals move? After each discussion and demonstration, try saying the new rhyme and moving in the new way.

6

Six Sensational Sounds

My father he died, but I can't tell you how;
He left me six horses to drive in my plough;
With my <u>wing</u>, <u>wang</u>, <u>waddle O</u>,
Jack sing <u>saddle O</u>,
<u>Blowsey boys</u> <u>bubble O</u>,
Under the broom.

Recite the rhyme for the children. Practice it. Explain that the human voice is an exciting musical instrument. We can make a wide range of sounds. Have fun making lots of different sounds with the voice. Then assign each child one of the six underlined sounds from the rhyme. Let children with the same sound meet and practice making the sound in an interesting way with their voices. See which group can invent the most unique sounds. Assemble together and recite the rhyme again as each group contributes its sound at the appropriate time. Let each group teach the others how they made the sound, and allow time for everyone to make all six sounds and perform the rhyme.

Six-Vegetable Soup

Discuss vegetables with your class. Make a list on the chalkboard of all of the vegetables they can name. Then ask each child what her favorite vegetable is. Vote to determine the six most favorite vegetables of your class. Make a Six Favorite Vegetables Graph. Ask everyone to bring one of the six most favorite vegetables to school to make soup.

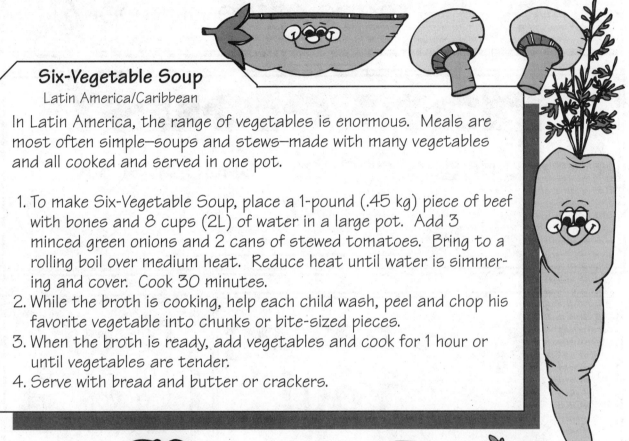

Six-Vegetable Soup
Latin America/Caribbean

In Latin America, the range of vegetables is enormous. Meals are most often simple—soups and stews—made with many vegetables and all cooked and served in one pot.

1. To make Six-Vegetable Soup, place a 1-pound (.45 kg) piece of beef with bones and 8 cups (2L) of water in a large pot. Add 3 minced green onions and 2 cans of stewed tomatoes. Bring to a rolling boil over medium heat. Reduce heat until water is simmering and cover. Cook 30 minutes.
2. While the broth is cooking, help each child wash, peel and chop his favorite vegetable into chunks or bite-sized pieces.
3. When the broth is ready, add vegetables and cook for 1 hour or until vegetables are tender.
4. Serve with bread and butter or crackers.

Sensational!

_____

knows the shape of the number **6**.

Marvelous!

You understand the concept of **six**.

To: _____

Amazing You!

You know that six is half of a dozen.

To: _____

Terrific!

I'm proud of the work you did with the number six.

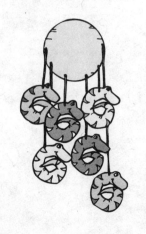

To: _____

Good Sitting in the Egg Center,

_____ !

You know the number pairs that total six.

7 seven

Solomon Grundy,
Born on Monday,
Christened on
    Tuesday,
Married on
    Wednesday,
Took ill on Thursday,
Worse on Friday,
Died on Saturday,
Buried on Sunday.
This is the end of
Solomon Grundy.

Monday's child is fair of face,
Tuesday's child is full of grace,
Wednesday's child is full of woe,
Thursday's child has far to go,
Friday's child is loving and giving,
Saturday's child works hard for its living,
But the child that's born on the Sabbath day
Is bonny and blithe, and good and gay.

As I was going to St. Ives,
I met a man with seven wives,
Every wife had seven sacks,
Every sack had seven cats,
Every cat had seven kits:
Kits, cats, sacks and wives,
How many were going to St. Ives?

Solomon Grundy

Solomon Grundy,
Born on a Monday,
Christened on Tuesday,
Married on Wednesday,
Took ill on Thursday,
Worse on Friday,
Died on Saturday,
Buried on Sunday.
This is the end of
Solomon Grundy.

Count to seven. Show the children seven fingers. Count each one. Explain that there are seven days in the week. Say the days of the week, and let the students count them. Use the rhyme as a choral reading as follows:

All:
Solomon Grundy
Child 1:   *Born on a Monday,*
Child 2:   *Christened on Tuesday,*
Child 3:   *Married on Wednesday,*
Child 4:   *Took ill on Thursday,*
Child 5:   *Worse on Friday,*
Child 6:   *Died on Saturday,*
Child 7:   *Buried on Sunday.*
All: *This is the end of Solomon Grundy.*

Calendar Crafts

Preschoolers do not need to learn the order of the days of the week or even be able to name them all, but working with calendars is a good way to introduce the concept of seven days. Give each student a blank calendar and a page of stickers on page 120. Write the name of the month at the top of each calendar. Students are to cut and paste the numbers on the calendar in numerical order. Show the children where to put the numeral one on their calendars according to the month you are celebrating.

Sunday	Monday	Tuesday	Wednesday	Thursday	Friday	Saturday

Calendar Crafts

Children can color each number sticker and draw pictures on special days like birthdays or holidays.

1	2	3	4	5	6	7
8	9	10	11	12	13	14
15	16	17	18	19	20	21
22	23	24	25	26	27	28
29	30	31				

Seven Cats

As I was going to St. Ives,
I met a man with seven wives,
Every wife had seven sacks,
Every sack had seven cats,

Every cat had seven kits:
Kits, cats, sacks and wives,
How many were going to St. Ives?

Which sack has seven cats? Circle it.

TLC10011 Copyright © Teaching & Learning Company, Carthage, IL 62321

Seven Sacks

As I was going to St. Ives,
I met a man with seven wives,
Every wife had seven sacks,
Every sack had seven cats,
Every cat had seven kits:
Kits, cats, sacks and wives,
How many were going to St. Ives?

Getting Ready: Stimulate learning with a smell center. Place different aromatic foods or plants in seven lunch-sized sacks. Cut a sniff hole (a hole big enough to put a nose in but small enough so you cannot see inside) in each sack. Number the sacks one through seven and place in the learning center. Reproduce the worksheet on the following page and place in the center. Change the objects in the sacks often.

Objective: Children are allowed to sniff each bag seven times to distinguish aromas. They complete the worksheet by drawing a picture of what they think is inside each of the seven bags.

Variation: Instead of using worksheets, pictures of the seven foods or plants that are in the sacks may be placed at the center, and children match the pictures with the corresponding sack.

Examples of Objects to Place in Sacks:
    slice of onion or garlic
    rose or other aromatic blossom
    slice of lemon or lime
    slice of apple or orange
    banana
    cinnamon stick or vanilla beans
    chocolates
    coffee beans or tea bags
    cotton ball soaked in perfume or men's cologne
    pine branches
    popped corn or peanuts

Seven Sacks

1.

2.

3.

4.

5.

6.

7.

Name _____

A Sack of Seven Kittens

As I was going to St. Ives,
I met a man with seven wives,
Every wife had seven sacks,
Every sack had seven cats,
Every cat had seven kits:
Kits, cats, sacks and wives,
How many were going to St. Ives?

Look in magazines to find pictures of cats or kittens. Cut and paste seven cats or kittens in the sack. If you cannot find enough pictures of cats, you may draw some.

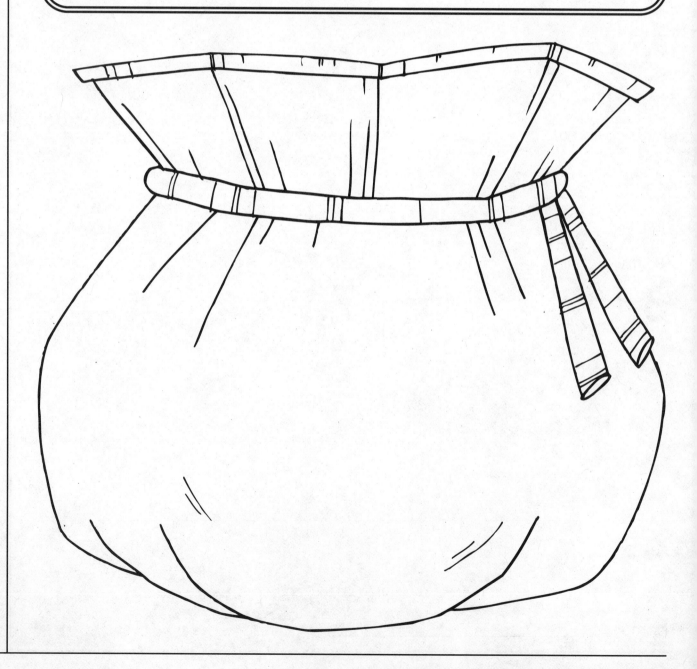

Treasure Chest of Shells

Cut out the two parts of the treasure chest, front and back. Paste along the edges and bottom of the back of chest and place front of chest on top to form a pocket. Let paste dry. Cut out the seven shell stamps. Color the treasure chest and shells. Practice putting the shells in numerical order from one to seven. When you are not working with the shell cards, keep them in the treasure chest.

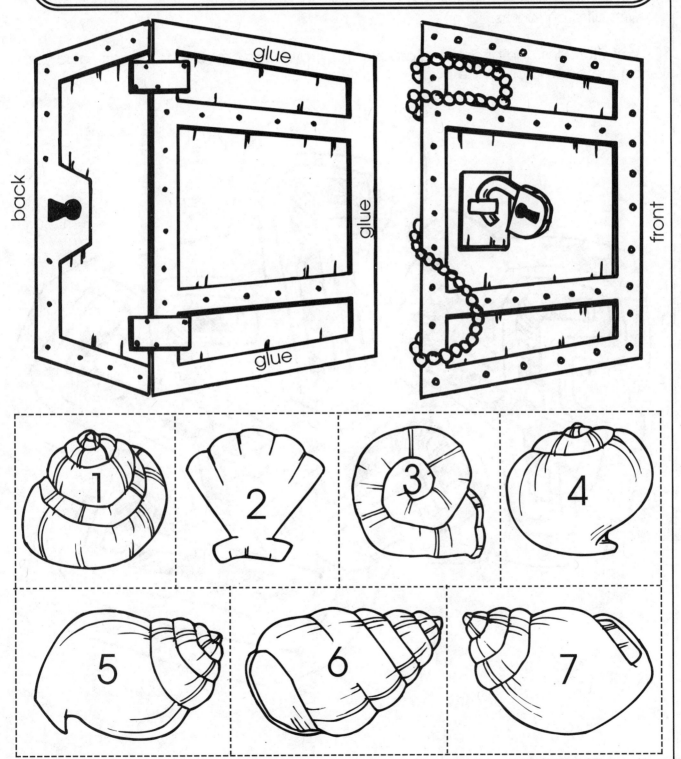

Seven-Straw Sculpture

Flex straws are perfect for creating three-dimensional sevens. Bend the straw and hold the short side down to make the shape of the numeral seven. Have the children bend a straw and make the numeral seven. Then give each student seven straws. Have them bend and attach each straw below to create an abstract three-dimensional design. Straws can overlap each other and should be placed randomly. Glue each straw on the paper and let dry. When dry, outline straws with different colors.

Variation: Instead of drawing around the straws with crayons or markers, glue yarn on the page around the edges of straw.

St. Ives Rummy

As I was going to St. Ives,
I met a man with seven wives,
Every wife had seven sacks,
Every sack had seven cats,
Every cat had seven kits:
Kits, cats, sacks and wives,
How many were going to St. Ives?

Getting Ready: Mount rummy cards on light cardboard or heavy paper. If the cards are going to be used over and over, laminate or cover with clear adhesive paper. Cut along dotted lines.

Directions: This game is for 2 to 4 players. It is played like a simple version of Gin Rummy. Shuffle cards and deal each player seven cards. Place the other cards facedown in a stack. The top card is turned faceup. The first player can take the card turned faceup or draw from the top of the stack. Then he discards one card. The next player can take the top card or the card that has been discarded. Players take turns drawing and discarding until one player can make a set of four matching cards plus a set of three matching cards. Cats cannot be matched with kittens. There are two wild cards–a man and a road to St. Ives card; these cards may be used with any other cards when making sets. The first player with a set of three and a set of four matching cards is declared the winner.

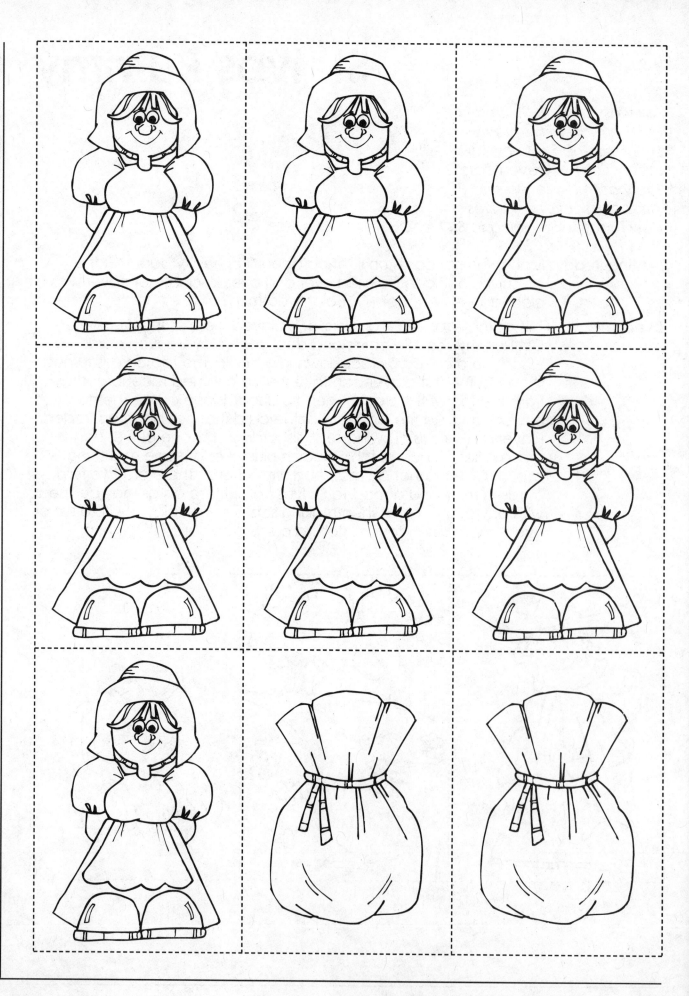

Game 7

Seven Sounds to Substitute

As I was going to St. Ives,
I met a man with seven wives,
Every wife had seven sacks,
Every sack had seven cats,
Every cat had seven kits:
Kits, cats, sacks and wives,
How many were going to St. Ives?

Recite the rhyme. Assign sounds as listed below for seven words in the rhyme. Ask a child or pair of children to make each of the sounds when they hear the appropriate word mentioned in the rhyme. Perform the rhyme as a participation story.

I	(Point to self and say, "That's me.")
going	(Slap knees and make walking sounds.)
man	(Point to someone else and say, "That's him.")
seven	(Count to seven.)
wives	(Say, "Yes, Dear.")
cats	(Purr like a cat.)
kits	(Meow.)

As I ("That's me.") *was going* (Slap knees with hands.) *to St. Ives,*
I ("That's me.") *met a man* ("That's him.") *with seven* (1, 2, 3, 4, 5, 6, 7)
    wives ("Yes, Dear."),
Every wife ("Yes, Dear.") *had seven* (1, 2, 3, 4, 5, 6, 7) *sacks,*
Every sack had seven (1, 2, 3, 4, 5, 6, 7) *cats* (Purr.),
Every cat (Purr.) *had seven* (1, 2, 3, 4, 5, 6, 7) *kits* (Meow.):
Kits (Meow.), *cats* (Purr.), *sacks and wives,*
How many were going to St. Ives?

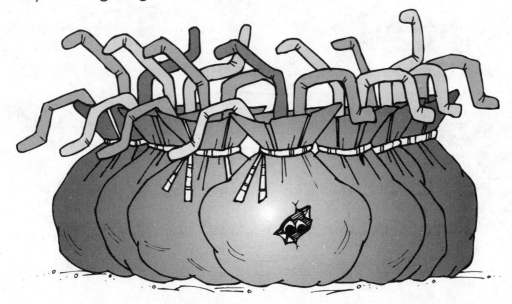

Dramatic Play

Seven-Layer Sandwich

Sandwiches are a delicious and nutritious way to eat all four food groups at once–bread, vegetables, meat, cheese. The sandwich was named for John Montague, Fourth Earl of Sandwich, who was born in 1718. It is said that he invented the sandwich as a timesaving nourishment while engaged in a twenty-four-hour gambling session. A 1950s cartoon character named *Dagwood Bumstead* made multilayered sandwiches an American tradition.

Dagwood Sandwich
United States

1. Slice a loaf of French bread lengthwise. On the bottom slice, layer the following:
   a. lettuce leaves
   b. sliced ham
   c. sliced American cheese
   d. sliced salami or pepperoni
   e. sprouts
   f. sliced tomatoes
   g. sliced Swiss cheese
2. Make sure each layer is thick enough to show the beautiful color layers of the meat, cheese and vegetables.
3. Spread condiments on the top slice of bread, and place on top of the sandwich. Cut into 8 to 12 pieces.

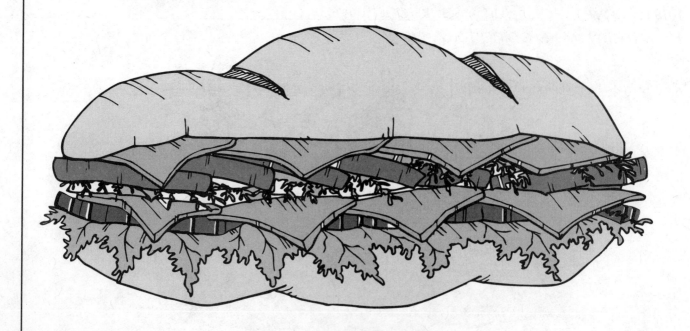

TLC10011 Copyright © Teaching & Learning Company, Carthage, IL 62321

Certificate of Award

_____

knows the shape of the number **7**.

Congratulations!

You understand the concept of **seven**.

To: _____

Sensational!

I'm certainly proud of the work you did with the number seven.

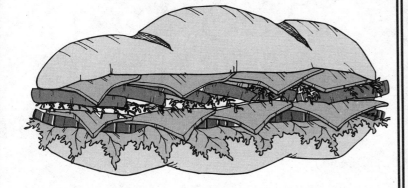

To: _____

Commendable!

You can count to seven.

To: _____

8 eight

One, two, three, four,
Mary at the cottage door;
Five, six, seven, eight,
Eating cherries
    off a plate;
O-U-T spells
    out!

Cantaloupes! Cantaloupes!
What is the price?
Eight for a dollar,
And all very nice.

Cherries on a Plate

One, two, three, four,
Mary at the cottage door;
Five, six, seven, eight,
Eating cherries off a plate;
*O-U-T spells **out**!*

Count to eight. Show the children eight fingers. Count each one. Draw a row of eight cherries on the chalkboard. As children sit with eyes closed, erase some cherries. Ask a student to come up and draw the needed cherries to have a total of eight. Repeat giving each child a turn to draw cherries on the chalkboard.

Variation: Give each pair of children a paper plate and eight paper cherries. (See the pattern above.) As one child closes her eyes and recites the rhyme, the other child removes some cherries from the plate and places them behind her back. At the end of the rhyme, the child counts the cherries that remain on the plate and guesses how many cherries have been removed. Count cherries to check answers. Then students switch places. Serve fresh cherries or cherry candies to culminate the activity. Each child gets eight, of course!

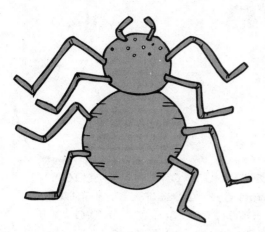

Eight Hairy Legs

Spiders have two distinct body sections that resemble the numeral eight. They have eight legs and often eight eyes. Use clay to make spider bodies. Talk about how the spider bodies look like fat numeral eights. Stick eight pipe cleaners in the sides of the clay bodies to make the spider's legs. Spiders have a pair of legs on each side of both body sections. Demonstrate how the legs should be positioned on the spider's body. Eyes can be added by poking indentations in the wet clay. When the clay hardens, bend the legs like spider legs as shown above.

Eight Cherries on My Plate

One, two, three, four,
Mary at the cottage door;
Five, six, seven, eight,
Eating cherries off a plate;
*O-U-T spells **out**!*

Draw the number of cherries you need to make eight on each plate.

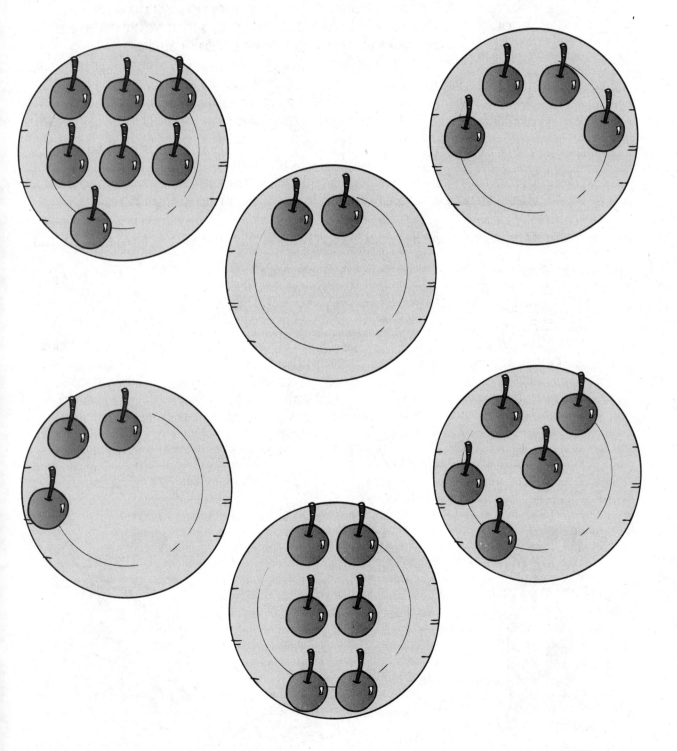

TLC10011 Copyright © Teaching & Learning Company, Carthage, IL 62321

Eight Things to Feel

Learning Center

Cantaloupes! Cantaloupes!
What is the price?
Eight for a dollar,
And all very nice.

Getting Ready: Place a cantaloupe at the center with an invitation to close eyes and feel the texture. Discuss the way a cantaloupe feels. Also place eight large grocery bags with a feel hole (a hole big enough to place hand inside but not so big that you can see inside the bag) cut in the middle of each as illustrated. Put a different fruit in each bag, and secure with yarn or string. Green fruit that isn't ripe yet is best so it won't get squished or messy in the bags. Number the bags one through eight. Place worksheets (page 139) at the learning center. Change objects in bags often.

Objective: Children place one hand in feel hole and touch the fruit at the bottom of bag. By feeling the size, texture, weight, etc., students try to identify the fruit in each bag. Complete the worksheets by drawing a picture of what is inside each numbered bag.

Variation: Vegetables or common household objects may be used instead of fruit.

Fruits to Place in Bags	Vegetables	Objects
apple	carrot	spatula
orange	lettuce or cabbage	book
lemon or lime	cauliflower	towel
cherries or grapes	peas in a pod	old computer disk
banana	corn on the cob	tape
pear	onion or garlic	flowerpot
peach or apricot	potato	spoon
melon	dried beans or peas	can of food
papaya or mango	peanut	glue stick
coconut	yams or sweet potato	cotton balls
gooseberries or blueberries	Brussels sprouts	paintbrush
tangerine or tangelo	rice	hammer
nectarine	green beans	sponge

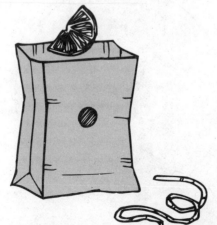

Eight Things to Feel

1.

5.

2.

6.

3.

7.

4.

8.

Name _____

Pretzel Stick Measuring

Use pretzel sticks to measure each of the following to the nearest whole number. Write your answers on the blanks.

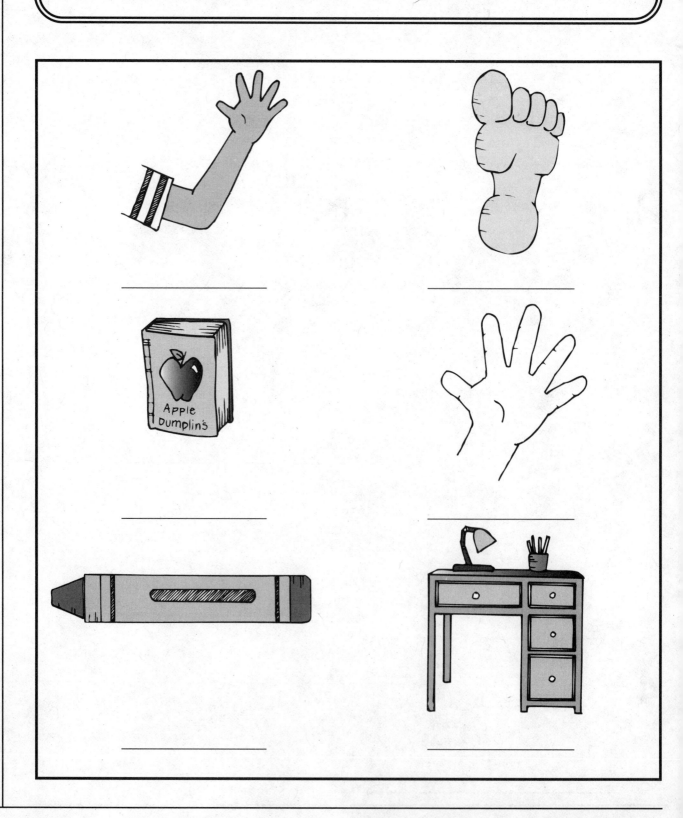

Eight Cantaloupes

Cantaloupes! Cantaloupes!
What is the price?
Eight for a dollar,
And all very nice.

Color the spaces with two dots green. Color the spaces with eight dots orange.

Cut and Paste

Building an Eight-Brick Chimney

Cut out the eight bricks at the bottom of the page. Matching the number words and numerals, paste each brick on the chimney. Color the pig and bricks.

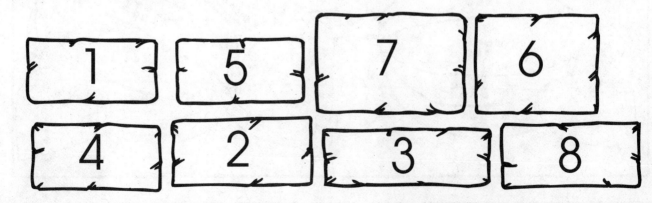

TLC10011 Copyright © Teaching & Learning Company, Carthage, IL 62321

Edible Pretzel Eights

Use frozen bread dough to make eight-shaped pretzels. Give each child a small ball of thawed bread dough. Roll into a rope and fashion into an eight shape. Place on an aluminum foil-covered baking sheet. Scratch each student's initials on the aluminum foil next to his pretzel. Sprinkle with salt. Cover and let rise one hour. Bake until brown and crusty on the outside.

Group Rope Jumping

One, two, three, four,
Mary at the
*   cottage door;*
Five, six, seven,
*   eight,*
Eating cherries
*   off a plate;*
*O-U-T spells **out**!*

Getting Ready: Sometimes it is easier for children to learn how to jump rope if they don't have to concentrate on turning their own rope. Use two children at either end of a long jump rope as turners. Help the turners learn how to turn the rope with a slow, steady beat. Sometimes it helps if the teacher is at one end of the rope as a turner.

Directions: Children line up and take turns running in and jumping four times for each line of the rhyme. After reciting O-U-T, the jumper runs out, and a new runner jumps in. Jumping rope is a good out-of-doors game, but in case of bad weather, it can be played inside a large room.

One,/two,/three,/four,

Mary/at the/cottage/door;

Five,/six,/seven,/eight,

Eating/cherries/off/a plate;

O/-U/-T/spells *out*!

Variation: Use the rhyme below to jump rope, too. Jump on each two or three syllables as indicated by underlined words.

Cantaloupes!/Cantaloupes!

What is/the price?

Eight for a/dollar,

And all/very nice.

O-N-E Spells *One*

One, two, three, four,
Mary at the cottage door;
Five, six, seven, eight,
Eating cherries off a plate;
O-U-T spells **out**!

Use the rhyme to practice spelling the number words one through eight. Each time you recite the last line, spell a number. Example: o-n-e spells 1!, t-w-o spells 2, etc. Hold up a different number card for each verse.

Dramatic Play

o-n-e 1

t-w-o 2

t-h-r-e-e 3

f-o-u-r 4

f-i-v-e 5

s-i-x 6

s-e-v-e-n 7

e-i-g-h-t 8

Eight Cherry Dishes

One, two, three, four,
Mary at the cottage door;
Five, six, seven, eight,
Eating cherries off a plate;
O-U-T spells **out**!

Cherry Salad
United States

Mix 1 large can of cherry pie filling with 1 small package of miniature marshmallows and 1 small box of instant vanilla pudding. Stir. Chill to set.

Cherry Sundae
United States

Place a scoop of vanilla ice cream in a small cup. Spoon a serving of cherry pie filling over the top. Dot with whipped cream.

Cherry Rice Pudding
Hungary

To make a quick cherry rice pudding, make 4 cups (960 ml) of instant rice. Let cool. Stir in a can of cherry pie filling. Stir and chill again.

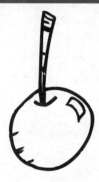

Cherry Cake
New Zealand

Make meringue shells and fill them with cherry pie filling.

1. Beat 6 egg whites until stiff.
2. Slowly add 6 ounces (170.1 g) of sugar to the stiff egg whites. Add 1/4 teaspoon (1.25 ml) vanilla and 1 teaspoon (5 ml) light malt vinegar and stir.
3. Pour into foil cupcake tins and make indentation in center.
4. Bake in the center of the oven for 1 1/2 hours at 275°F (135°C). When lightly brown, remove and let cool.
5. Put 1-2 tablespoons (15-30 ml) of cherry pie filling in each.

Eight Cherry Dishes

Cherry Pie
United States

Children can make quick, easy pies in class with already-made pastry shells and cherry pie filling.

1. Place pastry crust in glass pie pan and partially bake at 400°F (204°C) for 15 minutes. Remove from oven and cool.
2. Pour 1 can of pie filling in half-baked shell and top with another already-made pie crust. Pinch edges to seal the pie. Carve a large numeral eight in the top crust!
3. Bake for 25 more minutes or until top crust is brown.

Cherry Sauce
Israel

Wash 2 pounds (.9 kg) of cherries. Remove pits and coarsely chop. Place cherries, juice from 1 lemon and 1 thin strip lemon rind in a slow cooker. Add 2 tablespoons (30 ml) sugar and 1/4 cup (60 ml) water. Cover and cook on high about an hour until cherries are a pulp. Rub through a sieve or mash. Add 1 tablespoon (15 ml) butter. Beat well. Cool and chill. To make cherry butter, cook fruit another hour or until cherries are as thick as jam. Cool and chill.

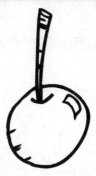

Cherry Cheesecake
United States

Use a prepared cheesecake mix. Follow directions to make the cheesecake. When set, pour a can of cherry pie filling on top. Serves 8 to 12.

Cherry Chocolate Cake
Germany

For a quick cherry cake, use a prepared chocolate cake mix. Follow directions. Bake in a round mold for 1 hour at 375°F (191°C) or until a knife inserted in cake center comes out clean. When cool, pour cherry pie filling over cake.

TLC10011 Copyright © Teaching & Learning Company, Carthage, IL 62321

Extraordinary!

_____

knows the shape of the number **8**.

Excellent!

You understand the concept of **eight**.

To: _____

I'm very proud of the excellent effort you have made with the number eight.

To: _____

How Exciting!

You can count to eight!

To: _____

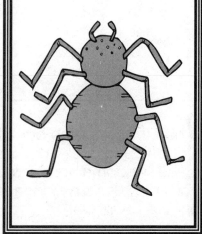

9 nine

Engine, Engine, Number Nine
Running on Chicago Line,
Please tell me the correct time.
One o'clock, two o'clock,
Three o'clock, four o'clock,
Five o'clock, six o'clock,
Seven o'clock, eight o'clock,
Nine!

Pease-porridge hot,
Pease-porridge cold,
Pease-porridge in the pot,
Nine days old.

Piping hot!
Smoking hot!
What have I got you have not?
Hot gray peas, hot, hot, hot,
Hot gray peas, hot. Hot!
(How many "hots" have I got?)

As I went over Lincoln Bridge,
I met Mister Rusticap;
Nine nice needles on his back,
A-going to Thorney Fair.

When the fox came back to his den,
He had young ones both nine and ten,
"You're welcome home, daddy; you may go again,
If you bring us such nice meat
From the town, Oh!"

150

Engine, Engine, Number Nine

Engine, Engine, Number Nine
Running on Chicago Line,
Please tell me the correct time.
One o'clock, two o'clock,
Three o'clock, four o'clock,
Five o'clock, six o'clock,
Seven o'clock, eight o'clock,
Nine!

Recite the rhyme with the children until they know the words. Then form two circles, with equal numbers of children, one inside the other. As they say the verse, the children in one circle walk around clockwise, the other counterclockwise. On the words *One o'clock*, they stop and shake hands with the person they are facing. Then they move to the next person and say, "Two o'clock." Continue moving and shaking hands until they reach "Nine." That person they hug. Then start the game all over and say the verse again. Repeat until the children tire of counting to nine and playing the game.

Nine Gum Balls

On heavy paper or light cardboard, reproduce the gum ball machine pattern below. Give each student a gum ball machine. Use large, adhesive multicolored dots to put exactly nine gum balls in the machine. Let each child choose the number of each color of gum balls. Share each completed machine. Count the different colors of gum in each child's machine. For example: How many red gum balls are in Pasha's gum ball machine? How many green gum balls does Tyler have in his machine?

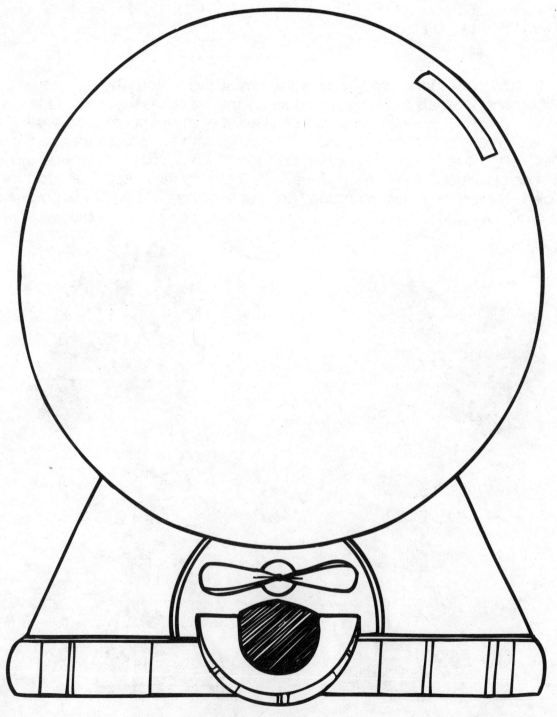

Nine-Noodle Lunch

Who has nine noodles for lunch? Circle your answer.

Pinecone Porcupines

As I went over Lincoln Bridge,
I met Mister Rusticap;
Nine nice needles on his back,
A-going to Thorney Fair.

Getting Ready: Place a box of pinecones, clay or play dough, and pine needles plus scissors, glue and scraps of felt for porcupine eyes in the center. Molding material should be in tightly sealed containers. Put an oil cloth or plastic covering on table in the learning center. Provide the step-by-step picture directions below and on the next page for making porcupines and a completed porcupine sample for children to see.

Objective: Children make a pinecone porcupine with exactly nine pine needles on his back.

Step 1

Find a pinecone that you like.
Find the best way to lay it down. It should lay flat and not roll.

Pinecone Porcupines

Step 2

Cut out felt eyes and glue them to pinecone.
Let dry.

Step 3

Press clay into the back of
your porcupine.
Count nine pine needles,
and stick them in
the back of
your porcupine.

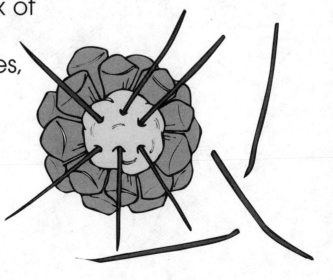

Nine Foxes in the Den

When the fox came back to his den,
He had young ones both nine and ten,
"You're welcome home, daddy; you may go again,
If you bring us such nice meat
From the town, Oh!"

Hidden in the picture with the fox are his young ones. Find and color the hidden baby foxes. Did you find nine?

Dialing for Numbers

Cut out each number word stamp at the bottom of the page. Matching the number words and numerals, paste each number word over the appropriate numeral on the telephone.

Cut and Paste

six	seven	three	four	two

eight	one	nine	five	zero

Nine Hot Gray Peas

Look at the verse below. Count the peas used in the words where *O*s should go. Use a gray crayon to turn the nine peas into nine number nines.

Piping h**o**t!
Smoking h**o**t!
What have I got
you have not?
H**o**t gray peas,
h**o**t, h**o**t, h**o**t,
H**o**t gray peas,
h**o**t. H**o**t!

Counting Peas Card Game

Pease-porridge hot,
Pease-porridge cold,
Pease-porridge in the pot,
Nine days old.

Getting Ready: Reproduce cards (pages 160-164) on heavy paper or light card-board. Color the cards as follows. Color one set of cards 0-9 red. Color another set blue, another set yellow and the fourth set green. You should have a set of ten red cards, ten yellow cards, ten blue cards and ten green cards, each with a different number. Cut apart. For more durability, laminate or cover with clear adhesive paper.

Directions: This card game can be played by two or three players. Shuffle cards and deal seven to each player. Place the rest of the cards facedown in the center of players. The object of the game is to collect two sets of cards: a set of four cards with the same number or the same color and a set of three cards with the same number or color. First player draws a card. He looks to see if the card will improve his hand. If the card will not improve his hand, he discards it faceup. The next player can draw the card on the top of the deck or take the last card that was discarded. If there are no more cards to select from, the discard pile is shuffled and placed facedown again. The game continues until one player has made two sets of cards with the same number or the same color.

Game

Counting Peas Card Game

0

0

0

0

1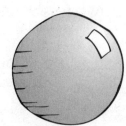

1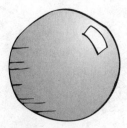

1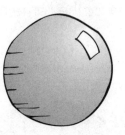

1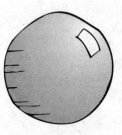

Counting Peas Card Game

2

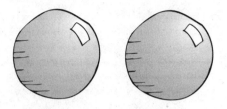

2

2

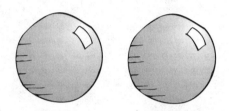

2

3

3

3

3

Counting Peas Card Game

  4

  4

4

4

5

5

5

5

Counting Peas Card Game

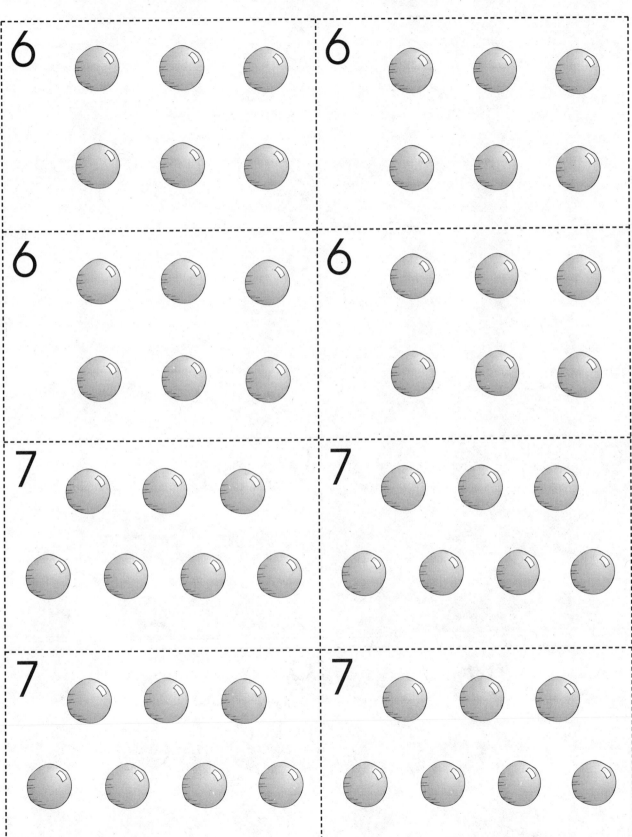

Counting Peas Card Game

8

8

8

8

9

9

9

9

Mother Nature's Instruments

Pease-porridge hot,
Pease-porridge cold,
Pease-porridge in the pot,
Nine days old.

There are many musical instruments to be found in nature. Take a walk outside. Challenge the children to find different things made by Mother Nature that can be used to make sounds. See the list of examples below. Then let everyone collect something to use as a musical instrument. When you return to the classroom, practice singing the rhyme using the instruments to keep time. Encourage students to make up tunes for some of the other rhymes they have learned, and use the instruments to accompany their songs.

Examples:
1. tree branches (beat together)
2. rock cymbals (clang together)
3. shell horns (punch a hole in one end and blow other end)
4. grass whistles (blow across to vibrate)
5. dry gourds (shake like rattles)
6. hollow reed whistles (make a hole in side and blow in one end)
7. rough wood blocks (rub together like sand blocks)
8. dry leaves (crunch and stir)
9. pine needle branches (swish)

Can you think of any more?

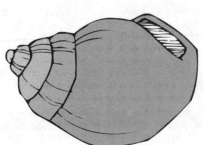
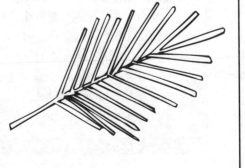

Dramatic Play

Pease-Porridge

Pease-porridge hot,
Pease-porridge cold,
Pease-porridge in the pot,
Nine days old.

Here are two recipes using peas. One is a hot dish, and the other is a cold one.

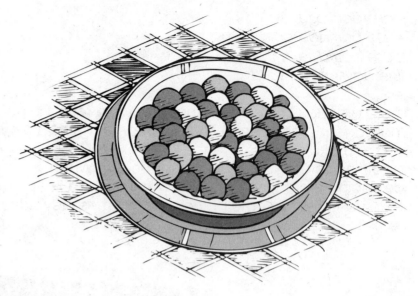

Creamed Peas

1. Cook 2 16-ounce (907.2 g) packages of frozen baby peas in ¼ cup (60 ml) water until tender. Drain off water.
2. In a small bowl, combine 1 cup (240 ml) milk, 2 tablespoons (30 ml) butter, 2 tablespoons (30 ml) sugar and 1 tablespoon (15 ml) cornstarch. Stir until blended. Pour over peas. Cook over low heat until sauce bubbles and thickens.
3. Serve with bread and butter.

Pea, Cashew and Ham Salad

1. In a medium bowl, combine ⅓ cup (80 ml) mayonnaise, ⅓ cup (80 ml) sour cream and the juice of a lemon. Mix to blend.
2. Stir in 1 16-ounce (453.6 g) package of thawed frozen peas, 2 cups (480 ml) diced cooked ham, ⅓ cup (80 ml) cashews and 1 8-ounce (226.8 g) can sliced water chestnuts. Stir. Chill.
3. On a cutting board with a serrated plastic knife, let children shred a head of lettuce. Place lettuce in plastic bowls. Place a scoop of salad on each bed of lettuce. Top with a few cashews.

Nice!

_____

knows the shape of the number **9**.

Nifty!

You can count to **nine**.

To: _____

Great Pinecone Porcupine

To: _____

Thank You,

_____,

for your continued good work with numbers.

To: _____

Ten, Do It Again

1, 2, 3, 4, 5!
Once I caught a fish alive;
6, 7, 8, 9, 10!
I let him go again.

Little Jack Horner
Sat in a corner,
Eating a Christmas pie;
He put in his thumb,
And pulled out a plum,
And said, "What a good boy am I!"

Dance, Thumbkin, dance;
Dance, ye merrymen, everyone;
For Thumbkin he can dance alone,
Thumbkin he can dance alone.

Dance, Foreman, dance;
Dance, ye merrymen, everyone;
But Foreman he can dance alone,
Foreman he can dance alone.

Dance, Longman, dance;
Dance, ye merrymen, everyone;
For Longman he can dance alone,
Longman he can dance alone.

Dance, Ringman, dance;
Dance, ye merrymen, dance;
But Ringman cannot dance alone,
Ringman he cannot dance alone.

Dance, Littleman, dance;
Dance, ye merrymen, dance;
But Littleman he can dance alone,
Littleman he can dance alone.

Cackle, cackle, Madam Goose!
Have you any feathers loose?
Truly have I, little fellow,
Half enough to fill a pillow;
And here are quills, take one or ten,
And make from each, pop-gun or pen.

10 ten

*Ten silly elephants standing in a line–
One ran away and then there were nine.
Nine silly elephants sitting on a gate–
One went for hay and then there were
   eight.
Eight silly elephants counting to eleven–
One saw a mouse and then there were
   seven.
Seven silly elephants picking up sticks–
One built a house and then there were
   six.
Six silly elephants looking at a hive–
One chased a bee and then there were
   five.

Five silly elephants dancing on the floor–
One bumped his knee and then there
   were four.
Four silly elephants sitting in a tree–
One fell out and then there were three.
Three silly elephants wearing something
   blue–
One gave a shout and then there were
   two.
Two silly elephants sitting in the sun–
One went swimming and then there was
   one.
One silly elephant looking for some fun–
Went to join the circus and then there
   were none!

A certain young farmer of Ayr,
Started with some sheep for the fair.
He reached the new bridge of Dover,
And, leaving his sheep, went over.
At the end of the bridge is an inn,
Where often before he had been;
Of the inns in the town 'twas the best,

And the farmer said, "Here I will rest."
The number of sheep was so great,
So narrow, too, was the sheep-gate,
That to get them all over, and where
Was resting the farmer of Ayr,
Will take us nine days, maybe ten;
The story must stop until then.

*With respect to the Ten Little Indians.

Ten Dancing Fingers

Recite the rhyme below with the children. Count all ten fingers. Show students the appropriate finger actions for each line of the rhyme. As they listen or join in the recitation, move fingers accordingly.

Dance, Thumbkin, dance;   (Tuck in fingers, wiggle thumb.)
Dance, ye merrymen, everyone;   (Wiggle all fingers and thumbs.)
For Thumbkin he can dance alone,   (Wiggle only the thumbs.)
Thumbkin he can dance alone.   (Wiggle only the thumbs.)

Dance, Foreman, dance;   (Wiggle only index fingers.)
Dance, ye merrymen, everyone;   (Wiggle all fingers and thumbs.)
For Foreman he can dance alone,   (Wiggle only index fingers.)
Foreman he can dance alone.   (Wiggle only index fingers.)

Dance, Longman, dance;   (Wiggle only middle fingers.)
Dance, ye merrymen, everyone;   (Wiggle all fingers and thumbs.)
For Longman he can dance alone,   (Wiggle only the thumbs.)
Longman he can dance alone.   (Wiggle only the thumbs.)

Dance, Ringman, dance;   (Wiggle only ring fingers.)
Dance, ye merrymen, everyone;   (Wiggle all fingers and thumbs.)
For Ringman he cannot dance alone,   (Wiggle only ring fingers.)
Ringman he cannot dance alone.   (Wiggle only ring fingers.)

Dance, Littleman, dance;   (Wiggle only little fingers.)
Dance, ye merrymen, everyone;   (Wiggle all fingers and thumbs.)
For Littleman he can dance alone,   (Wiggle only little fingers.)
Littleman he can dance alone.   (Wiggle only little fingers.)

Feather Print Goose

Cackle, cackle, Madam Goose!
Have you any feathers loose?
Truly have I, little fellow,
Half enough to fill a pillow;
And here are quills, take one or ten,
And make from each, pop-gun or pen.

Printing is an interesting art project, and usually the results
are quite pleasing. Begin this project by reproducing the
goose pattern on page 172 on gray or light blue construc-
tion paper for each student. Have the children dip feathers in paint and carefully
press on paper. Practice the technique of printing with a feather on scratch
paper until students can get just enough paint and pressure on feather to make a
clear print. Then use white or gray paint and a feather to stamp exactly ten feather prints on each paper goose. Let the paint dry. Cut out the goose. Mount on
green construction paper. Count the feather prints on each goose.

Variation: Use the tip of the feather to paint. Instead of mounting the goose on
green paper, glue it to a sheet of white paper. Dip the tip of the feather in green
paint, and draw squiggly lines around the base of the goose to represent grass.

Feather Print Goose

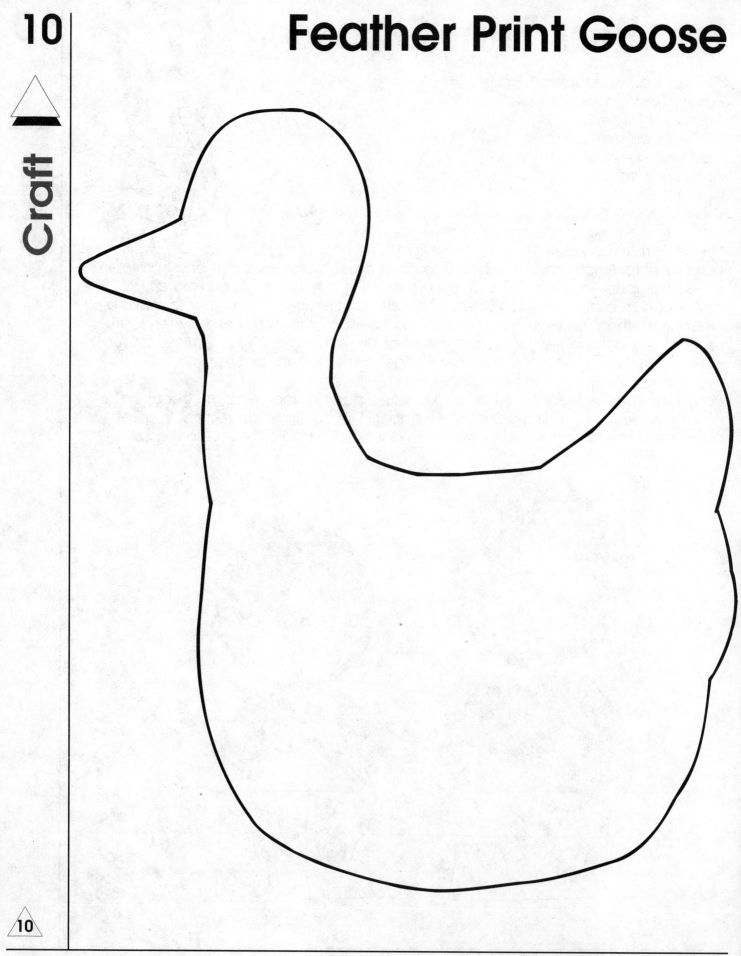

Ten Silly Elephants

To see all ten silly elephants, cut out the puzzle pieces below. Put the puzzle together, and then glue each piece in place on another sheet of paper.

Ten Clay Fish

1, 2, 3, 4, 5!
Once I caught a fish alive;
6, 7, 8, 9, 10!
I let him go again.

Learning Center

Getting Ready: A sculpting center provides a good place to practice eye-hand skills. Place clay, play dough or molding material of your choice in tightly sealed containers. Put an oil cloth or plastic covering on a table in the learning center.

Objective: Children are to mold ten little fish. Pictures of fish or a live fish in an aquarium should be in the center so the children can see how fish are shaped. When the fish have been sculpted, place them in a prominent place with a copy of the rhyme.

Variation: To reinforce the number ten, children can mold their own hands with ten fingers or feet with ten toes. If they are sculpting feet, have the students remove their shoes to study their feet before beginning to sculpt. (Be sure to count ten fingers or toes!)

I Caught a Fish!

Write the correct number in each square to show how many fish there are.
Color the fish.

Number Farm

Can you find the numerals 0-10 hidden in the picture? Circle each numeral. Color the picture.

TLC10011 Copyright © Teaching & Learning Company, Carthage, IL 62321

Dial a Whale

To make a Dial a Whale, you will need scissors, crayons and a brad fastener. Cut out the wheel below. Mount the wheel on heavy paper or light cardboard. Trim around the edge. See the directions for the construction of the whale on the next page.

Games to Play: 1. Look at the window with a number word, and try to guess the numeral. Look in the little window to check your answer.

2. Look at the window with the numeral, and try to spell the matching number word.

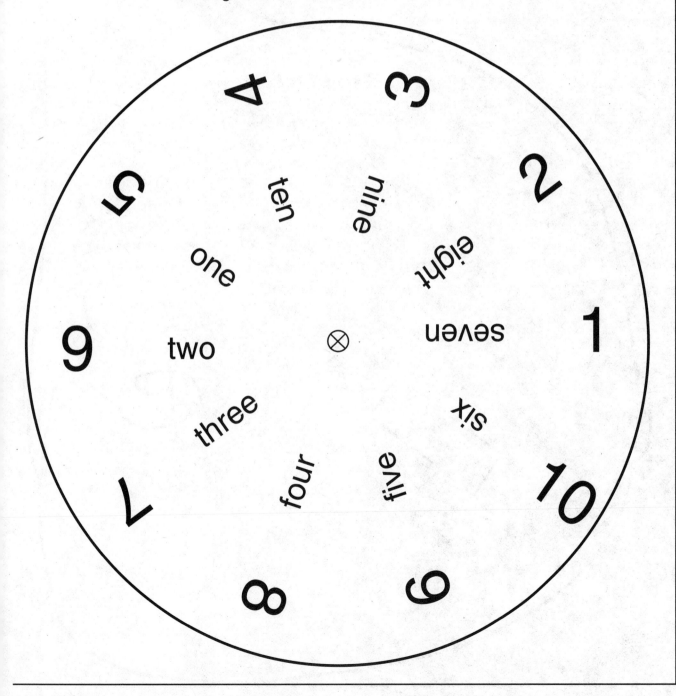

Dial a Whale

Cut and Paste

Directions:

1. Reproduce whale on heavy paper or light cardboard.

2. Cut out and color the whale.

3. Attach the wheel to the back of the whale with a brad fastener through the *X* in the center of the wheel and whale.

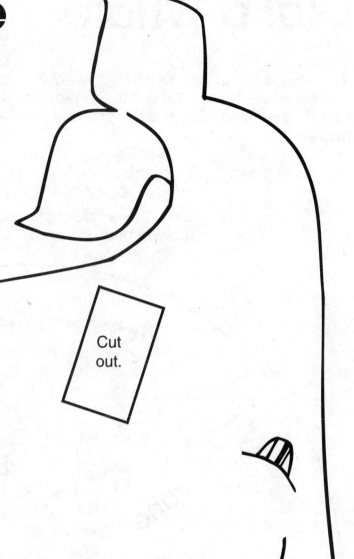

Cut out.

Cut out.

Christmas Plums

Little Jack Horner
Sat in a corner,
Eating a Christmas pie;
He put in his thumb,
And pulled out a plum,
And said, "What a good boy am I!"

Why did Jack pull out just one plum? He could have pulled out two cherries or seven bananas. Help children create their own verses by adding a fruit word (or anything else) and a last line to each verse. Allow plenty of time for the students to illustrate their stories. For example: Jack Horner pulled out five strawberries, eight apples or ten lemons. Then cut out the pages of each book and assemble them in order. Staple pages together, and make covers for the books.

Writing Idea

Little Jack Horner
Sat in a corner,
Eating a Christmas pie;
He put in his thumb,
And pulled out 2 limes,
And said, "I'll sell these to you
     for two dimes!"

Little Jack Horner
Sat in a corner,
Eating a Christmas pie;
He put in his thumb,
And pulled out 2 _____,
And said, " _____ ."

Writing Idea

Christmas Plums

Little Jack Horner
Sat in a corner,
Eating a Christmas pie;
He put in his thumb,
And pulled out 3 _____ ,
And said, " _____ ."

Little Jack Horner
Sat in a corner,
Eating a Christmas pie;
He put in his thumb,
And pulled out 4 _____ ,
And said, " _____ ."

Little Jack Horner
Sat in a corner,
Eating a Christmas pie;
He put in his thumb,
And pulled out 5 _____ ,
And said, " _____ ."

Little Jack Horner
Sat in a corner,
Eating a Christmas pie;
He put in his thumb,
And pulled out 6 _____ ,
And said, " _____ ."

Christmas Plums

Little Jack Horner
Sat in a corner,
Eating a Christmas pie;
He put in his thumb,
And pulled out 7 _____ ,
And said, " _____ ."

Little Jack Horner
Sat in a corner,
Eating a Christmas pie;
He put in his thumb,
And pulled out 8 _____ ,
And said, " _____ ."

Little Jack Horner
Sat in a corner,
Eating a Christmas pie;
He put in his thumb,
And pulled out 9 _____ ,
And said, " _____ ."

Little Jack Horner
Sat in a corner,
Eating a Christmas pie;
He put in his thumb,
And pulled out 10 _____ ,
And said, " _____ ."

Bridge of Dover

A certain young farmer of Ayr,
Started with some sheep for the fair.
He reached the new bridge of Dover,
And, leaving his sheep, went over.
At the end of the bridge is an inn,
Where often before he had been;
Of the inns in the town 'twas the best,
And the farmer said, "Here I will rest."
The number of sheep was so great,
So narrow, too, was the sheep-gate,
That to get them all over, and where
Was resting the farmer of Ayr,
Will take us nine days, maybe ten;
The story must stop until then.

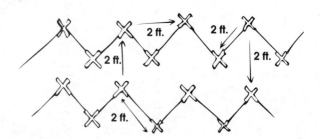

Getting Ready: On the asphalt, use chalk to draw a 2' (.61 m) wide obstacle course as illustrated. Put two lines of *X*s 2' (.61 m) apart, and then connect the *X*s on both sides. This is the Bridge of Dover.

Directions: One child is chosen to be the young farmer. Another child is the sheep. The other children stand on the lines of the obstacle course. Blindfold the sheep. The young farmer carefully guides his "sheep" through the course. The object is to get the sheep over the bridge without touching any of the children standing on the sidelines. Give everyone a chance to be both farmer and sheep.

Listen!

Ten silly elephants standing in a line—
One ran away and then there were nine.
Nine silly elephants sitting on a gate—
One went for hay and then there were eight.
Eight silly elephants counting to eleven—
One saw a mouse and then there were seven.
Seven silly elephants picking up sticks—
One built a house and then there were six.
Six silly elephants looking at a hive—
One chased a bee and then there were five.

Five silly elephants dancing on the floor—
One bumped his knee and then there were four.
Four silly elephants sitting in a tree—
One fell out and then there were three.
Three silly elephants wearing something blue—
One gave a shout and then there were two.
Two silly elephants sitting in the sun—
One went swimming and then there was one.
One silly elephant looking for some fun—
Went to join the circus and then there were none!

Directions: As teacher recites the rhyme, children show the appropriate number of fingers each time a number is mentioned. After going through the rhyme in order, mix up the lines from the rhyme as children listen and show the appropriate fingers.

The Fish Race

1, 2, 3, 4, 5!
Once I caught a fish alive;
6, 7, 8, 9, 10!
I let him go again.

Getting Ready: Reproduce pages 188 and 189. If you want more than one gameboard, reproduce these pages several times. Attach the gameboard halves to the inside of a file folder. Place colorful sticky dots along the gameboard path. Color the pictures on the gameboard. Laminate or cover with clear adhesive paper. For each game you wish to make, reproduce a set of game cards on pages 185-187. Cut apart cards. Place cards in a 6" x 8" (15.24 x 20.32 cm) manila envelope, and attach the envelope to the back of the file folder. Paste the game rules below on the cover of the file folder.

The Fish Race

This game can be played by 2 to 4 players.

Materials:
one game marker for each player
set of 63 game cards

Rules:
1. Place game markers in the "Go" space.
2. Shuffle the game cards, and place them facedown near the gameboard.
3. Take turns flipping over the top card and moving the number of spaces indicated by the card. If player cannot read the numeral or number word she lands on, she does not advance her marker and must return to the space where she started that turn.
4. Place card facedown on the bottom of the deck.
5. The first player to cross the finish line is declared the winner!

The Fish Race

File Folder Game

0	1	2
4	5	6
8	9	10
3	7	3
5	6	7
9	10	2
8	9	7

10

The Fish Race

zero	one	two
four	five	six
eight	nine	ten
seven	two	three
five	six	seven
nine	ten	zero
one	two	three

The Fish Race

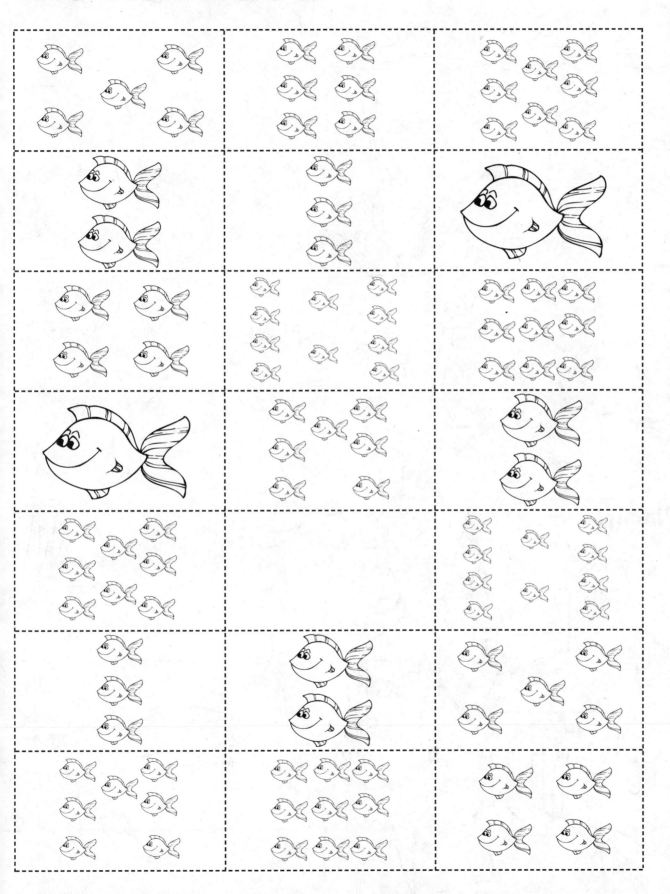

File Folder Game

Go

Finish

File Folder Game

Ten Silly Elephants

The Ten Silly Elephants rhyme can be used as a short play. Ten children stand in a line and recite the verse. At the end of each line, one child does the indicated action and leaves the line. See the play script and suggested actions on page 191.

Create colorful paper headbands to wear during the play. Cut headband to fit around head and staple to make it to fit snugly. Cut long (about 36" x 1" (.30 m x 2.54 cm)) strips of paper, and tape or paste ends together as shown.

Ten Silly Elephants

Ten silly elephants standing in a line—
One ran away and then there were nine.
> *(Waves good-bye and walks off stage)*

Nine silly elephants sitting on a gate—
One went for hay and then there were eight.
> *(Rubs tummy and lopes off stage)*

Eight silly elephants counting to eleven—
One saw a mouse and then there were seven.
> *(Pantomimes seeing a mouse and runs off stage)*

Seven silly elephants picking up sticks—
One built a house and then there were six.
> *(Pantomimes building and leaves stage)*

Six silly elephants looking at a hive—
One chased a bee and then there were five.
> *(Pantomimes seeing and chasing a bee and leaves stage)*

Five silly elephants dancing on the floor—
One bumped his knee and then there were four.
> *(Dances, drops to one knee, pantomimes pain and limps off stage)*

Four silly elephants sitting in a tree—
One fell out and then there were three.
> *(Falls to floor and crawls off stage)*

Three silly elephants wearing something blue—
One gave a shout and then there were two.
> *(Yells to off stage and leaves stage)*

Two silly elephants sitting in the sun—
One went swimming and then there was one.
> *(Pantomimes getting out of chair and diving into water, swims off stage)*

One silly elephant looking for some fun—
Went to join the circus and then there were none!
> *(Pirouettes and prances off stage)*

Ten Plump Plums Pie

Little Jack Horner
Sat in a corner,
Eating a Christmas pie;
He put in his thumb,
And pulled out a plum,
And said, "What a good boy am I!"

Open pies, sometimes called tarts, are popular in Germany and are made with a variety of fruits. Plums and apples are the most common fruits used in German pies.

Plum Pie

Germany

1. Dissolve ¹/2 ounce (14.17 g) dried yeast in 8 tablespoons (120 ml) milk. Add a pinch of sugar.
2. Put 1 pound (.45 kg) flour into a warm bowl, and make a hollow in the center of the flour. Add the yeast. Carefully mix into a pastry. Cover with a cloth and leave in a warm place about 30 minutes until it rises.
3. Soften ¹/3 cup (80 ml) butter. Mix butter with 2 tablespoons (30 ml) sugar, a pinch of salt, 1 teaspoon (5 ml) grated lemon rind, 8 tablespoons (120 ml) milk and 1 egg. Add this mixture to the risen pastry.
4. Knead in the bowl until the dough comes away from the sides of the bowl and is shining smooth. Sprinkle with flour. Cover and let rise again.
5. Preheat oven to 425°F (218°C). Roll out dough very thinly, and spread on a flat greased baking sheet. Sprinkle with sugar.
6. Let students wash and dry 2 pounds (.9 kg) ripe plums. Slit each plum and remove seed. Open each whole plum and lay flat on dough. Sprinkle with sugar again. Let rise one more time for 15 minutes. Bake in the oven for 30 minutes. Serves 8 to 12.

TLC10011 Copyright © Teaching & Learning Company, Carthage, IL 62321

Terrific!

_____

knows the shape of the number **10**.

Listen Up!

You understand the concept of **ten**.

To: _____

Very Good,

_____!

You can count to ten.

Great Work,

_____,

with the number ten.

11 eleven

Around the green gravel the grass grows green,
And eleven pretty maids are plain to be seen;
Wash them with milk, and clothe them with silk,
And write their names with a pen and ink.

Nature requires five,
Custom gives seven,
Sleepyheads take nine,
And laziness eleven.
 (hours of sleep)

Good horses, bad horses,
What is the time of day?
Three o'clock, four o'clock,
Five o'clock, six o'clock,
Seven o'clock, eight o'clock,
Nine o'clock, ten o'clock,
Eleven. Now fare you away.

Hickery, dickery, 6 and 7,
Wishbone, crackabone, 10 and 11.

Note: Some of these rhymes have been changed slightly to teach
the number eleven.

Wishbone, Crackabone, Clap, Clap, Clap

Hickery, dickery, 6 and 7,
Wishbone, crackabone, 10 and 11.

Clapping is a good way to teach young children to keep a beat. Begin by having students listen and count the number of claps they hear. Then give a number and the children clap that many times. Use the rhyme as follows to practice keeping the beat. Each time the verse is repeated, a clap replaces another word at the end of each sentence. Teacher may wish to put her index finger to lips to remind students when not to speak.

Hickery, dickery, 6 and 7,
Wishbone, crackabone, 10 and 11.

Hickery, dickery, 6 and (clap),
Wishbone, crackabone, 10 and (clap).

Hickery, dickery, 6 (clap, clap),
Wishbone, crackabone, 10 (clap, clap).

Hickery, dickery, (clap, clap, clap),
Wishbone, crackabone, (clap, clap, clap).

Hickery, (clap, clap, clap, clap),
Wishbone, (clap, clap, clap, clap).

(Clap, clap, clap, clap, clap).
(Clap, clap, clap, clap, clap).

Magician's Hat

To review counting from one to eleven, have each child make his own manipulative. Reproduce enough hats with the pattern below and strips on page 197 on construction paper or other heavy paper so that each child has his own set. Have students cut out the hat and strips. Glue the strips together end to end where indicated. Color animals on strip. Cut two slits in each hat where indicated. Insert strip and glue end to end to form a loop as illustrated. Children slide the strip around to reveal different groups of animals to count.

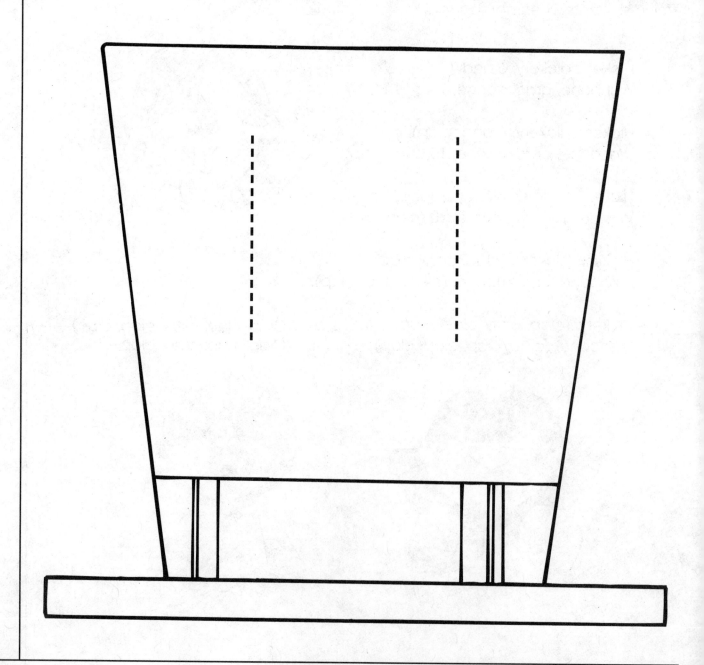

glue

glue

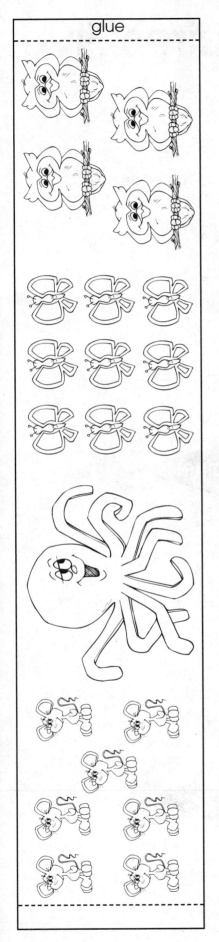

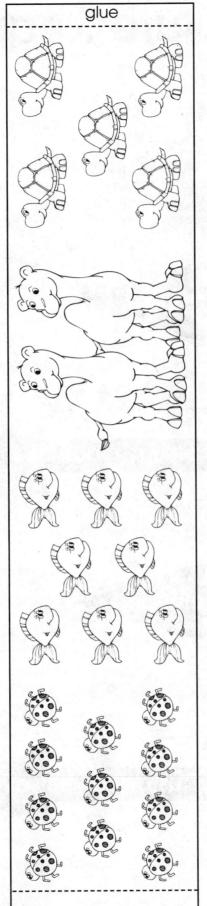

glue

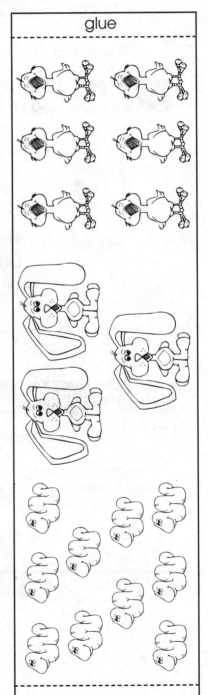

Nature Requires Five

Nature requires five,
Custom gives seven,
Sleepyheads take nine,
And laziness eleven.

Cut out the hands of the clock on this page and the clock on page 199. Glue each hand so it points to the correct hour.

Number Recognition

Nature Requires Five

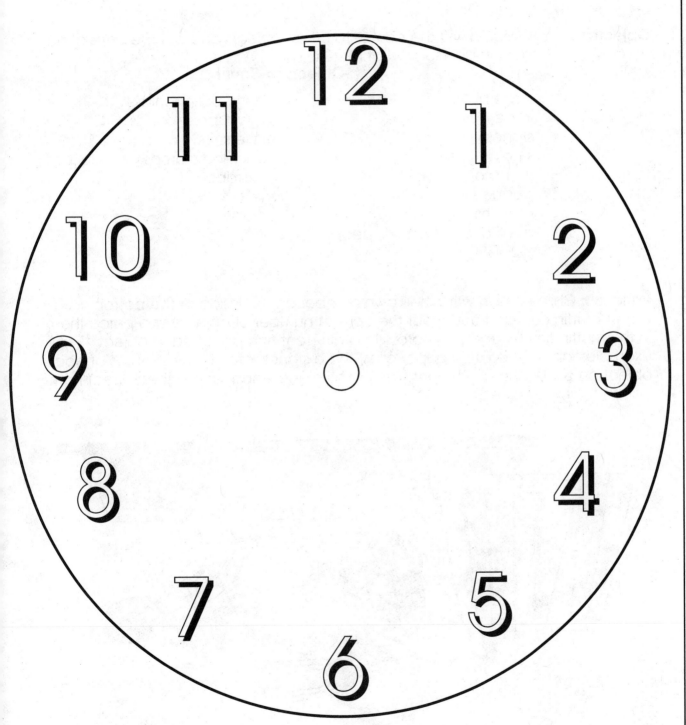

Number Sort

Getting Ready: Use muffin tins to sort and count small objects. Put 67 of any of the objects listed below in a bowl. Put a number 0-11 on a paper muffin cup, and place one in each section of the muffin tin.

Objective: Children visit the center to count objects and put the correct number in each section of muffin tins.

Objects to Count

large buttons
large paper clips
stones
small leaves
round dry cereal
peanuts in shells
crayons
small plastic animals, people,
cars

plastic poker chips
large rubber bands
erasers
canceled stamps mounted on
cardboard
shells
acorns

Variation: Children can write their own number on the inside of the bottom of a paper muffin cup and count out the correct number of objects and place them in the muffin tin. Or each day provide a different number of each object. For example: one button, two paper clips, three stones, etc. Draw pictures of each object on a worksheet. Students count the objects and record the correct number on their worksheets.

Please exercise caution when using small objects around small children.

Around the Green Gravel

Around the green gravel the grass grows green,
And eleven pretty maids are plain to be seen;
Wash them with milk, and clothe them with silk,
And write their names with a pen and ink.

Find the path through the maze that passes over the numbers 1-11 in the correct order. Color it green.

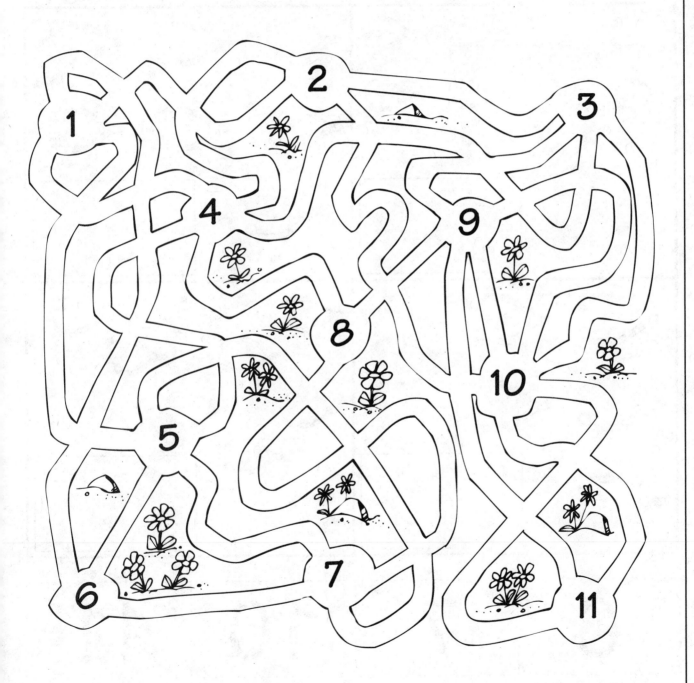

Wishbone, Crackabone, 10 and 11

Hickery, dickery, 6 and 7,
Wishbone, crackabone, 10 and 11.

Cut out the numeral stamps at the bottom of the page and glue them in the box with the same number of wishbones.

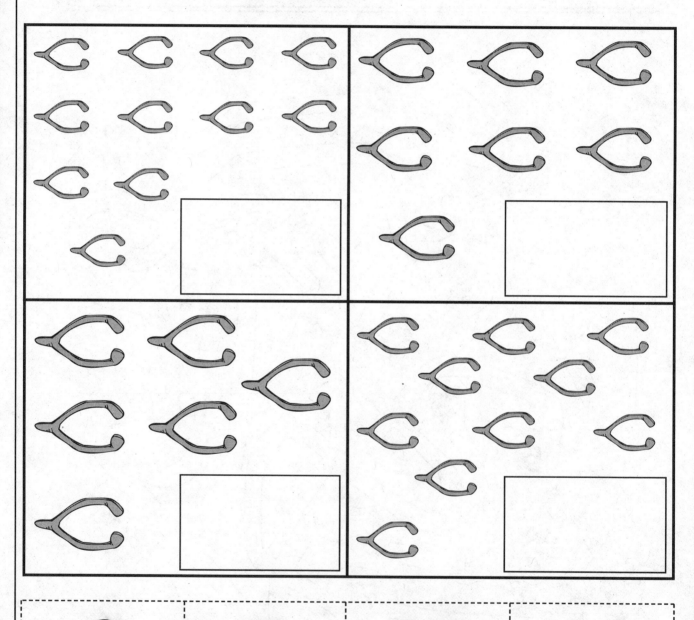

| 6 | 7 | 10 | 11 |

Number Mobile

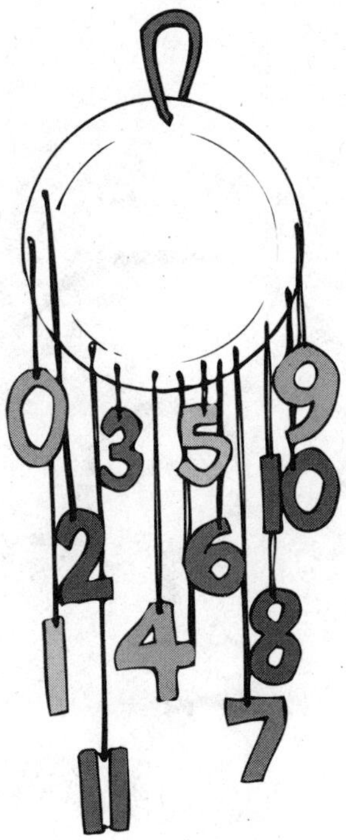

Cut out the numbers 0-11 on this page and pages 204 and 205. Outline each number with a black marker or crayon. Decorate each numeral with dots, stripes, flowers, etc. Punch a hole in each where indicated. Attach different lengths of yarn to each one. Punch twelve holes in a 12" (30.48 cm) paper plate. Attach the numbers to the paper plate as illustrated. Hang your number mobile where everyone can see it!

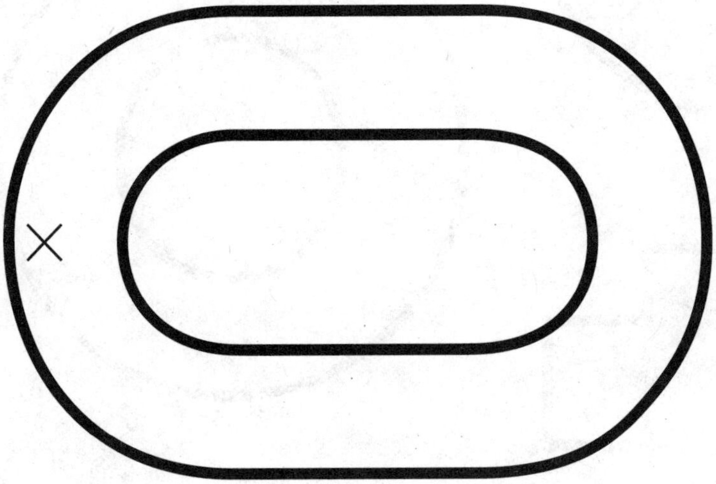

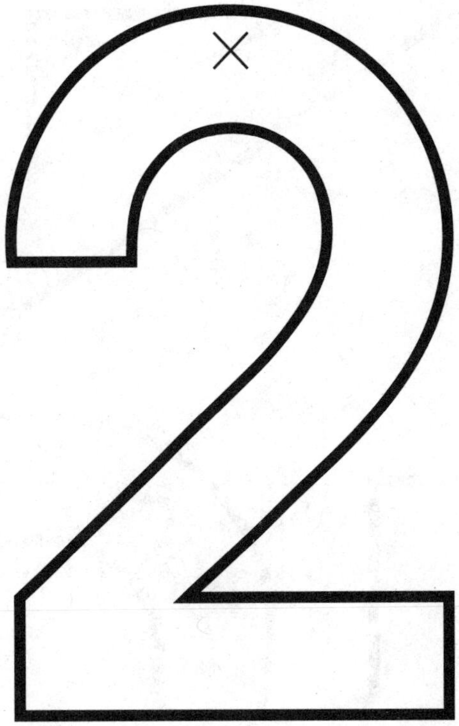

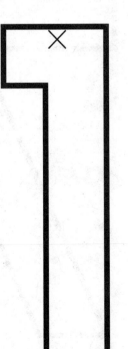

Number Mobile

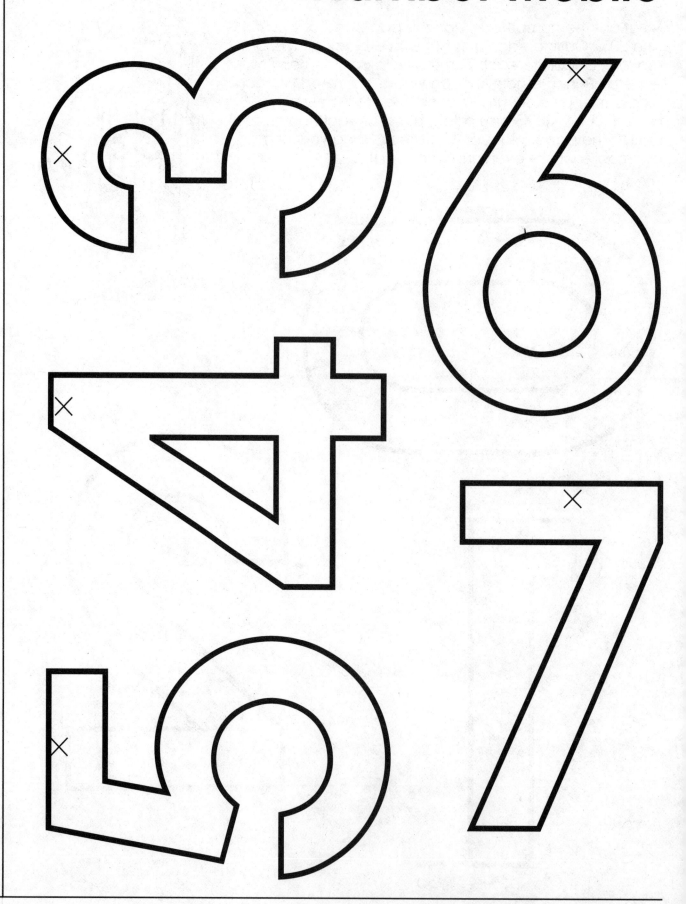

Number Mobile

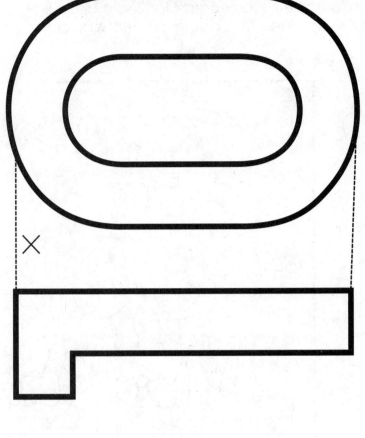
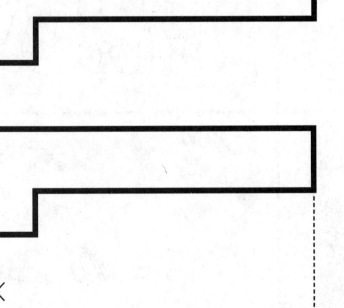
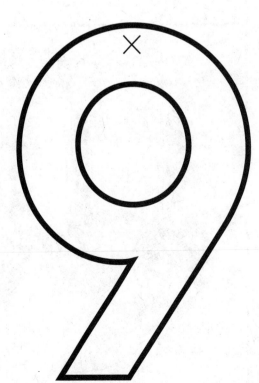

What's Missing?

Getting Ready: Cut out the cards on this page and pages 207 and page 208. Color each set of animals. To make sturdier cards, laminate or cover each with clear adhesive paper. See game directions on page 207.

What's Missing?

Directions: Show the children all twelve cards. Discuss that there is a different number of animals on each card. Place the cards on the chalkboard tray or another place where everyone can see them all at the same time. See rules on page 208.

11

What's Missing?

Rules: Ask students to close their eyes. Remove one card and rearrange the others. When the children open their eyes, they are to guess which set of animals is missing.

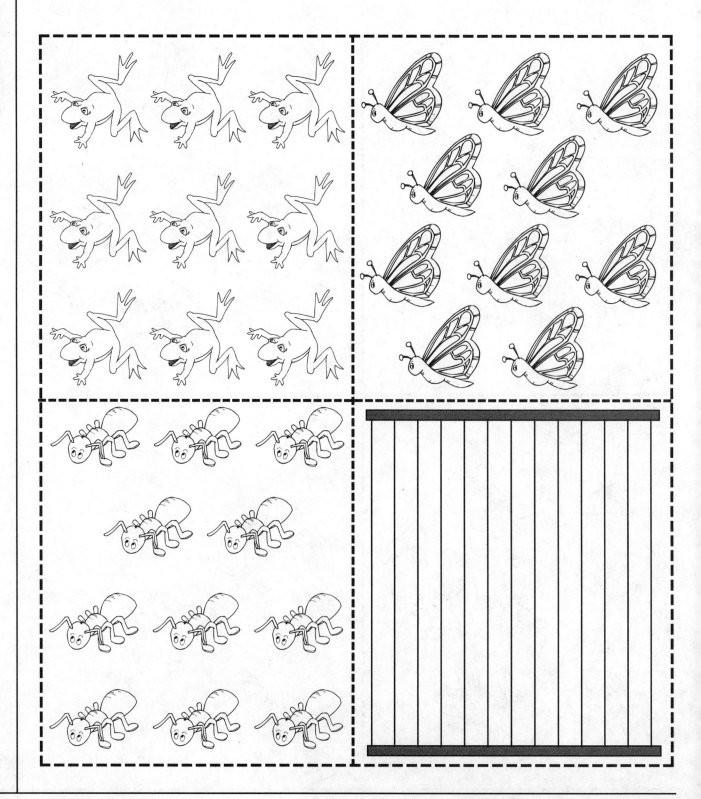

Around the Green Gravel

Around the green gravel the grass grows green,
And eleven pretty maids are plain to be seen;
Wash them with milk, and clothe them with silk,
And write their names with a pen and ink.

To turn this rhyme into a finger play, use the actions for each line below and sing it to the tune of "The Bear Went over the Mountain."

Around the green gravel
    (Hold palms down and horizontal. Use hands to draw circles.)
the grass grows green,
    (Wiggle fingers as if they are grass blowing in the wind.)
And eleven pretty maids
    (Put down one thumb and wiggle the other fingers and thumb.)
are plain to be seen;
    (Hold fingers and one thumb still so all can see each one.)
Wash them with milk,
    (Pretend to wash face.)
and clothe them with silk,
    (Pretend to button a blouse or shirt.)
And write their names
    (Pretend to write with an imaginary pen.)
with a pen and ink.
    (Hold up an imaginary pen.)

Wishbone Stew and Eleven Dumplings

Hickery, dickery, 6 and 7,
Wishbone, crackabone, 10 and 11.

Wishbone Stew
United States

1. In a large pot, cover a big stewing hen with water. Bring water to a boil, then cover with lid and reduce heat to a simmer. Cook for 2$^{1}/_{2}$ hours or until chicken falls away from the bone.
2. Remove chicken from broth and separate meat from skin and bones. Show the children the wishbone.
3. Place chicken meat back into broth.

Eleven Dumplings
Germany

1. Place 4 cups (960 ml) flour and 1 teaspoon (5 ml) salt into a large bowl.
2. Add 5 beaten eggs and mix thoroughly. Add only enough water to make a stiff, smooth batter. Do not over mix. Let rest for 15 minutes.
3. Use a spatula to lift dough onto a floured cutting board. Cut in half, then quarters. To make exactly eleven dumplings, cut each quarter except one into three pieces. Cut one quarter in half.
4. Count the dumplings as you drop each one into gently boiling broth and chicken. Cover and cook for 6-7 minutes or until done.
5. Remove chicken and dumplings. Thicken broth with 1 tablespoon (15 ml) of flour. Pour over chicken and dumplings.

Perfect!

_____

knows the shape of the number **11**.

Excellent!

You can count to **eleven**.

To: _____

Exceptional!

_____

can write the numbers 0 to 11.

Terrific Work

with the numbers 0 to 11!

To: _____

12 twelve

*Twelve little monkeys jumping
   on the bed.
One fell out and hurt his head.
The rest called the doctor,
And the doctor said,
"That is what you get for jumping
   on the bed."

I saw a peacock with a fiery tail,
I saw a blazing comet drop down hail,
I saw a cloud wrapped with ivy round,
I saw an oak creep on the ground,
I saw a snail swallow up a whale,
I saw the sea brimful of ale,
I saw a Venice glass full fifteen feet deep,
I saw a well full of men's tears that weep,
I saw red eyes all of a flaming fire,
I saw a house bigger than the moon and higher,
I saw the sun at twelve o'clock at night,
I saw the man that saw this wondrous sight.

I bought a dozen new-laid eggs,
Of good old farmer Dickens;
I hobbled home upon two legs,
And found them full of chickens.

*Adapted from "Five Little Monkeys."

12 twelve

One old Oxford ox opening oysters;
Two tee-totums totally tired of trying to trot to Tadbury;
Three tall tigers tippling tenpenny tea;
Four fat friars fanning fainting flies;
Five frippy Frenchmen foolishly fishing for flies;
Six sportsmen shooting snipes;
Seven Severn salmons swallowing shrimp;
Eight Englishmen eagerly examining Europe;
Nine nimble noblemen nibbling nonpareils;
Ten tinkers tinkling upon ten tin tinderboxes with tenpenny tacks;
Eleven elephants elegantly equipped;
Twelve typographical topographers typically translating types.

One, two, buckle my
   shoe;
Three, four, close the door;
Five, six, pick up sticks;
Seven, eight, stand up
   straight;
Nine, ten, ring
   Big Ben;
Eleven, twelve,
   dig and delve.

I Saw a Peacock

I saw a peacock with a fiery tail,
I saw a blazing comet drop down hail,
I saw a cloud wrapped with ivy round,
I saw an oak creep on the ground,
I saw a snail swallow up a whale,
I saw the sea brimful of ale,
I saw a Venice glass full fifteen feet deep,
I saw a well full of men's tears that weep,
I saw red eyes all of a flaming fire,
I saw a house bigger than the moon and higher,
I saw the sun at twelve o'clock at night,
I saw the man that saw this wondrous sight.

Read the rhyme to the children. Discuss what is wrong in each sentence. For example: Peacocks do not have fiery tails; comets have fiery, blazing tails. A cloud isn't wrapped in ivy, but sometimes an oak tree is wrapped in ivy. Explain that the rhyme actually is a riddle. If the punctuation is changed, the rhyme makes perfect sense. Reread it as follows:

I saw a peacock.
With a fiery tail, I saw a blazing comet.
Drop down hail, I saw a cloud.
Wrapped with ivy round, I saw an oak.
Creep on the ground, I saw a snail swallow.
Up a whale, I saw the sea.

Brimful of ale, I saw a Venice glass full.
Fifteen feet deep, I saw a well.
Full of men's tears that weep, I saw red eyes.
All of a flaming fire, I saw a house.
Bigger than the moon and higher, I saw the sun.
At twelve o'clock at night, I saw the man that saw this wondrous sight.

Variation: Ask the children to close their eyes and visualize some of the sights as you read the rhyme one last time.

Paper Chains

One, two, buckle my shoe;
Three, four, close the door;
Five, six, pick up sticks;
Seven, eight, stand up straight;
Nine, ten, ring Big Ben;
Eleven, twelve, dig and delve.

Creating paper chains is a good way to reinforce counting skills. Cut 2" x 6" (5.08 x 15.24 cm) paper strips from colorful construction paper. Have each student count twelve strips. Interlock paper links as illustrated. Glue the strips end to end. Let glue dry. Count the links in each chain. Paper chains may be made with particular colors to celebrate certain holidays. Hang the chains around the room.

Variation: Colorful designs can be incorporated into the chains by numbering links from 1 to 12 and having the children attach them in numerical order.

Patterns to Try

1. Every other link a different color.
   Odd numbers are one color.
   Even numbers are another color.

2. Every third link is the same color.
   Number pink links: 1, 4, 7 and 10.
   Number green links: 2, 5, 8 and 11.
   Number orange links: 3, 6, 9 and 12.

3. Every fourth link is the same color.
   Number red links: 1, 5 and 9.
   Number purple links: 2, 6 and 10.
   Number yellow links: 3, 7 and 11.
   Number black links: 4, 8 and 12.

One, Two, Buckle My Shoe

Count the objects in each row. Write the number in the box.

Number Recognition

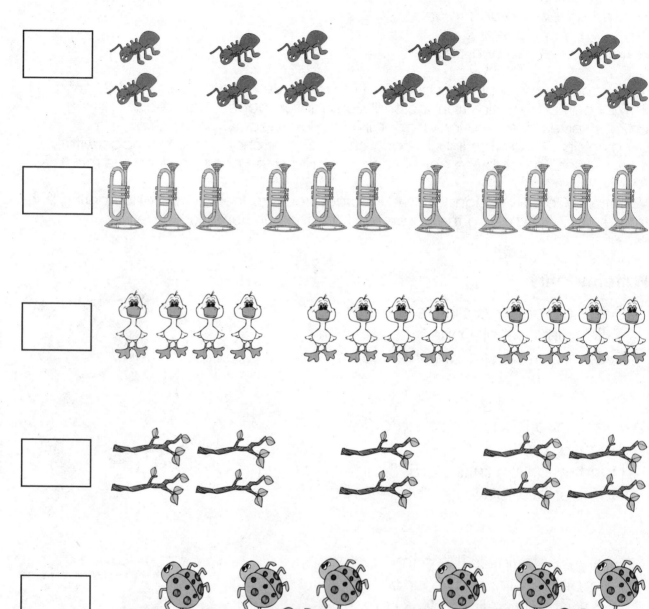

TLC10011 Copyright © Teaching & Learning Company, Carthage, IL 62321

Post Office Center

Getting Ready: A post office center is a good place to practice matching numerals. Shoe boxes decorated like little houses, or a large box with divided sections (like post office boxes) can serve as the basic center. In the center, place an assortment of different sized envelopes sealed with a number on the outside of each one. "Addresses" on envelopes should include 0 through 12. Number the boxes to match.

Objective: Children sort the mail and place envelopes in the matching post office box or shoe box house.

Variation: Give each student a number and prominently display it on his desk. That number is his "address." Children draw pictures or write short messages to each other and address them with the appropriate number. Place each letter in correct mailbox or decorated shoe box houses at the post office center.

12

217

Twelve Little Monkeys

Can you find twelve monkeys hiding in this picture? Circle them and color the picture.

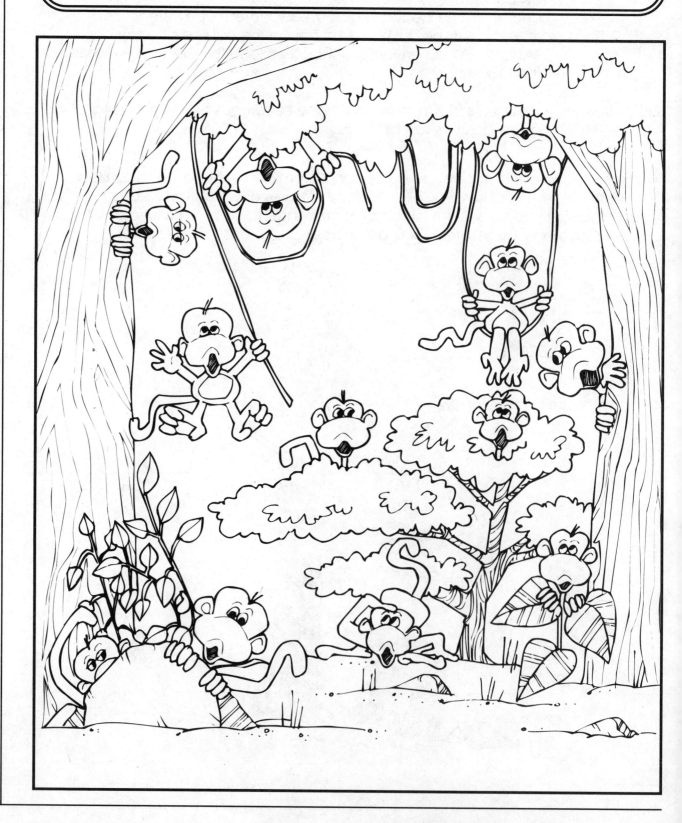

One, Two, Buckle My Shoe

One, two, buckle my shoe;
Three, four, close the door;
Five, six, pick up sticks;
Seven, eight, stand up straight;
Nine, ten, ring Big Ben;
Eleven, twelve, dig and delve.

Count the objects in each row. Draw a line to match them to the number in the box.

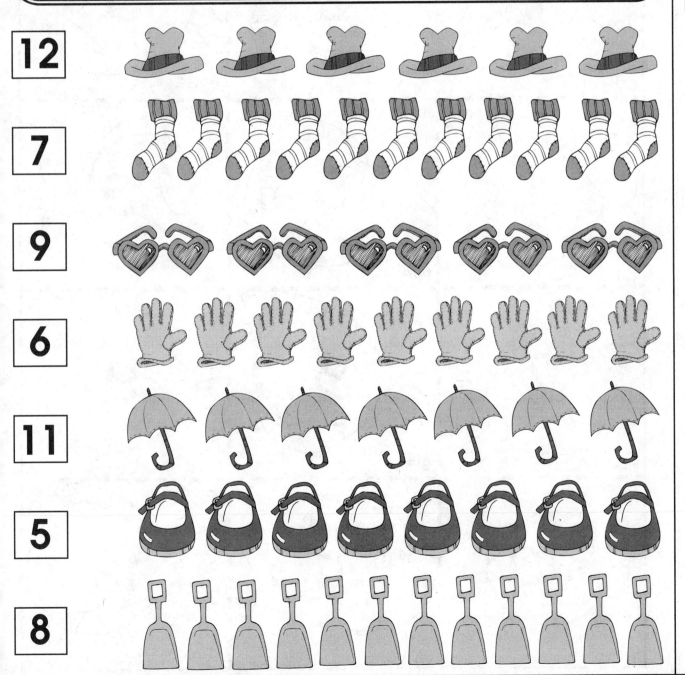

12

7

9

6

11

5

8

Fishy Mobile

Color each fish. Remember, fish can be many beautiful colors. Decorate the fish with spots, stripes and other designs. Cut out the fish stamps. Paste them in numerical order to a long piece of yarn. The number one should be first, and twelve will be last. Hang your fishing line where everyone can see it.

one

two

three

four

five

six

seven

eight

nine

ten

eleven

twelve

Little Monkeys
Flip Book

Twelve little monkeys jumping on the bed.
One fell out and hurt his head.
The rest called the doctor,
And the doctor said,
"That is what you get for jumping on the bed."

To make a flip book, cut out all of the pictures on this page and on pages 222-224. Be careful to cut on the dotted lines so the pages of your flip book will be even. Stack the pages in order and staple at the bottom. Flip the pages of the book quickly, and watch the monkeys jumping. (Teacher may want to cut pages apart using a paper cutter.)

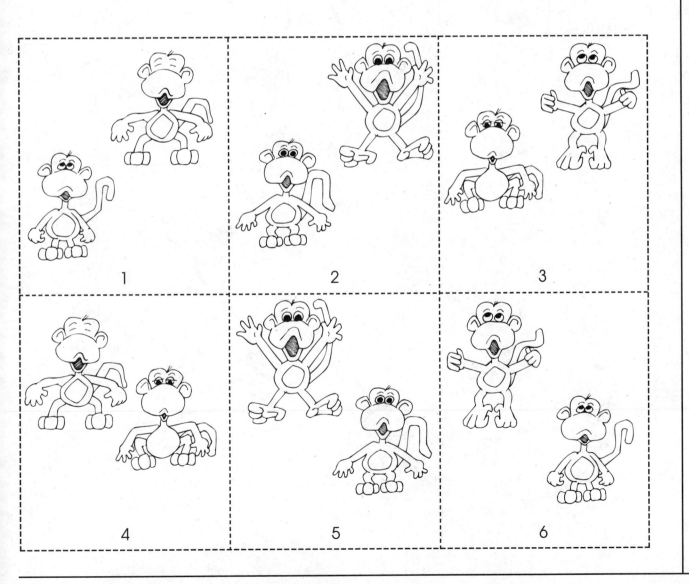

1

2

3

4

5

6

Little Monkeys Flip Book

7

8

9

10

11

12

13

14

15

Little Monkeys
Flip Book

Little Monkeys Flip Book

25

26

27

28

29

30

31

32

33

A Dozen Eggs

I bought a dozen new-laid eggs,
Of good old farmer Dickens;
I hobbled home upon two legs,
And found them full of chickens.

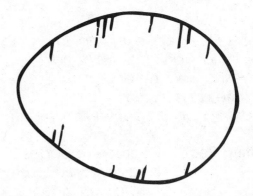

Getting Ready: Reproduce egg pattern above on different colors of construction paper. Cut out twelve paper eggs for each student. Give each student an empty egg carton.

Directions: Group children in pairs. Children take turns removing eggs form the carton and hiding them behind their backs. After looking at the carton, the partner guesses how many eggs have been removed. Count eggs to check work.

Variation: Write the numerals one to twelve on the eggs. Put the eggs in the carton in numerical order. Partners take turns removing one egg. The other child looks at the carton of eggs and guesses the number on the missing egg.

Monkeys' Marathon

Twelve little monkeys jumping on the bed.
One fell out and hurt his head.
The rest called the doctor,
And the doctor said,
"That is what you get for jumping on the bed."

Getting Ready: Reproduce pages 227 and 228. If you want more than one game-board, reproduce these pages several times. Attach the game-board halves to the inside of a file folder. Color the board. Cover with clear adhesive paper. Paste the game rules below on the cover of the file folder. If you wish, cover the front of the folder with clear adhesive paper, too.

Monkeys' Marathon

This game is for 2 to 4 players.
It is an active one.

Materials:
one game marker for each
    player
one die

Rules:
1. Place game markers in the "Go" space.
2. Roll the die to see who goes first. (Largest number goes first.)
3. Take turns rolling the die and advancing the number of spaces indicated.
4. When you land on a space, read or have someone read to you what it says to do. Then roll the die to see how many times you must do it. If you can perform the feat, you get to stay on that space. If you cannot perform the feat, you roll the die to see how many spaces you must move backwards.
5. Game continues until one monkey crosses the finish line.

File Folder Game

Go

Hop on one leg for _____ seconds.

Do _____ jumping jacks.

Do _____ push-ups.

Spell the number _____.

Name _____ sports.

Name your _____ best friends.

Sing the first _____ words of any song.

Walk backwards _____ steps.

Count from 20 to _____ backwards.

Spell your name _____ times fast.

Say a rhyme _____ times.

Hop backwards for _____ steps.

Count to 10 in _____ seconds.

Spell the number you roll backwards.

Take an extra turn.

Spell the number you roll.

Take an extra turn.

Bark like a dog _____ times.

Take an extra turn.

Hold your nose for _____ seconds.

Count to 20 _____ times.

Finish

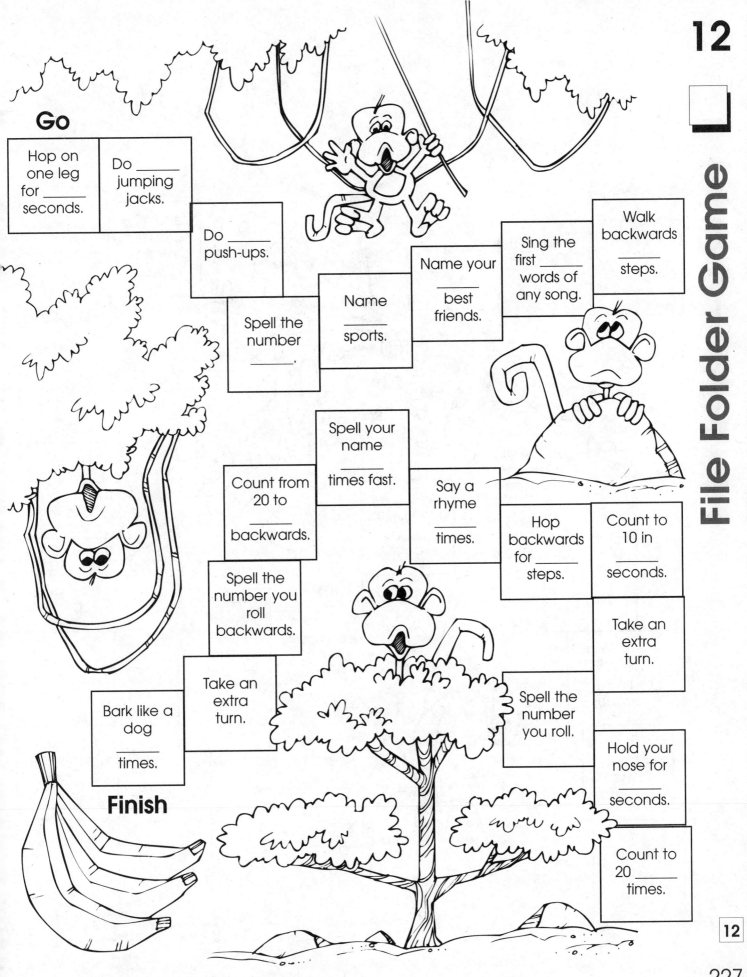

File Folder Game

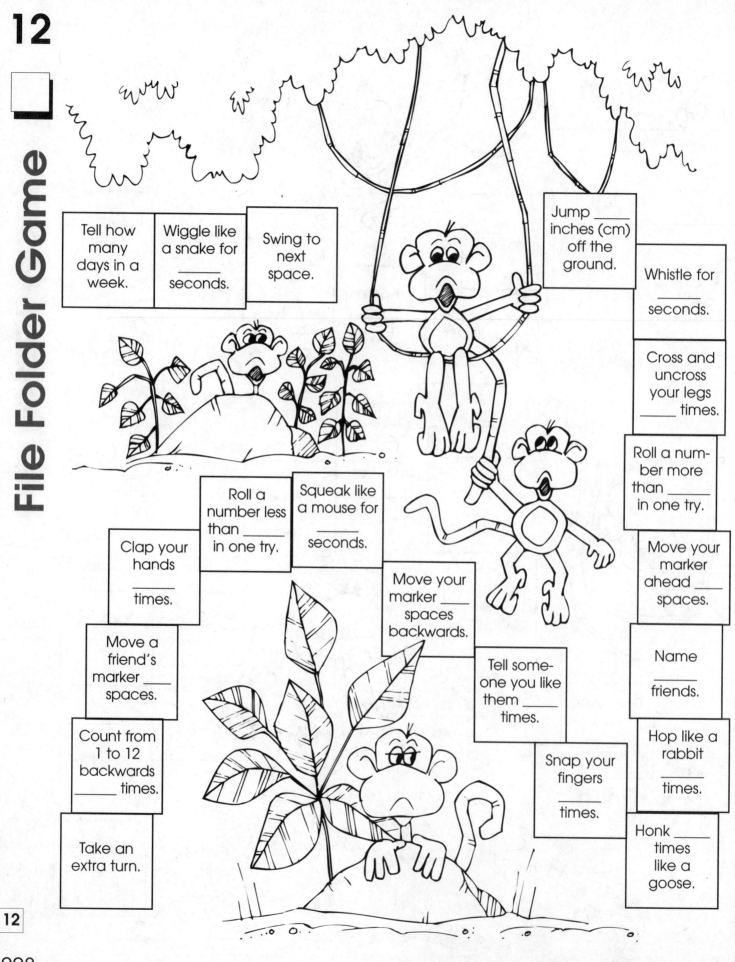

Tell how many days in a week.

Wiggle like a snake for _____ seconds.

Swing to next space.

Jump _____ inches (cm) off the ground.

Whistle for _____ seconds.

Cross and uncross your legs _____ times.

Roll a number more than _____ in one try.

Move your marker ahead _____ spaces.

Roll a number less than _____ in one try.

Squeak like a mouse for _____ seconds.

Clap your hands _____ times.

Move your marker _____ spaces backwards.

Tell someone you like them _____ times.

Name _____ friends.

Move a friend's marker _____ spaces.

Count from 1 to 12 backwards _____ times.

Snap your fingers _____ times.

Hop like a rabbit _____ times.

Take an extra turn.

Honk _____ times like a goose.

On the First Day of Summer

With minor adjustments, the rhyme, "I Saw a Peacock," can be sung to the tune of "Twelve Days of Christmas." The words are complicated so you may want to teach each line to individuals or pairs of children.

On the first day of summer, I saw such a sight,
A peacock with a fiery tail.
On the second day of summer, I saw such a sight,
A blazing comet,
On the third day of summer, I saw such a sight,
An ivy wrapped cloud,
On the fourth day of summer, I saw such a sight,
An oak creep on the ground,
On the fifth day of summer, I saw such a sight,
A snail swallow a whale,
On the sixth day of summer, I saw such a sight,
The sea full of ale,
On the seventh day of summer, I saw such a sight,
A glass fifteen feet deep,
On the eighth day of summer, I saw such a sight,
A well full of tears,
On the ninth day of summer, I saw such a sight,
Red eyes a-flaming,
On the tenth day of summer, I saw such a sight,
A house bigger than the moon,
On the eleventh day of summer, I saw such a sight,
The sun at night,
On the twelfth day of summer, I saw such a sight,
This wondrous sight.

Dramatic Play

One Dozen Egg Dishes

Recipes

I bought a dozen new-laid eggs,
Of good old farmer Dickens;
I hobbled home upon two legs,
And found them full of chickens.

Eggs in a Nest
United States

Cut a small circle out of the center of a piece of white bread. Place 1 tablespoon (15 ml) butter in a pan and heat. Put bread in pan and brown on one side. Turn. Break egg in the hole in the center of bread. Cover and cook until egg is set turning once if desired.

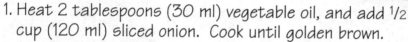

Egg Curry
India

1. Heat 2 tablespoons (30 ml) vegetable oil, and add ¹/2 cup (120 ml) sliced onion. Cook until golden brown.
2. Add 1 teaspoon (5 ml) turmeric, ¹/4 teaspoon (1.25 ml) curry, 6 thin slices fresh ginger and salt. Stir well. Slowly add 1 cup (240 ml) thick coconut milk. Cook 5 minutes.
3. Add another ¹/2 cup (120 ml) sliced onions. Stir.
4. Add 1 cup (240 ml) chicken broth and 1 tablespoon (15 ml) vinegar. Cook for 10 minutes.
5. Add 16 hard-boiled egg halves, and continue cooking for 10 minutes. Serve with rice.

Egg Salad
United States

1. Chop 8 hard-boiled eggs and place in a bowl.
2. Add 3 tablespoons (45 ml) salad dressing, 1 teaspoon (5 ml) mustard and 2 teaspoons (10 ml) sugar. Stir. Chill. Eat on bread or crackers.

One Dozen Egg Dishes

Breakfast Burrito

Mexico

On a flour tortilla place 2 tablespoons (30 ml) scrambled eggs and 1 tablespoon (15 ml) grated cheese. Microwave on high for 20 seconds. Serve with salsa.

French Toast

France

1. In a bowl, combine 6 eggs, 1/2 cup (120 ml) sugar, 4 tablespoons (60 ml) cinnamon and 1 teaspoon (5 ml) vanilla. Beat until fluffy.
2. Dip bread slices in egg mixture and fry in buttered skillet. Cook until bread is toasted on both sides. Serve with powdered sugar, syrup or jam.

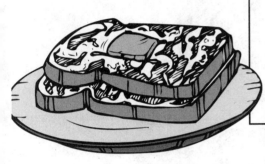

Irish Omelet

Ireland

1. Cube 4 large, boiled potatoes. Place in a bowl. Add 1/4 cup (60 ml) chopped green onion tops or chopped chives.
2. In another bowl, mix 8 eggs until fluffy. Pour over potatoes and stir.
3. Place 3 tablespoons (45 ml) butter in a pan and heat. Pour mixture into hot pan, place a lid on top and fry slowly until eggs are set. Can be topped with grated cheddar cheese.

One Dozen Egg Dishes

Recipes

Baked Eggs
USSR

1. Preheat oven to 200°F (93°C).
2. Line muffin pans with foil baking cups. In each place 1 teaspoon (5 ml) butter and 1 tablespoon (15ml) finely chopped ham.
3. Put one egg in each tin. Bake 15 minutes or until egg is cooked the way you like it.

Quiche Lorraine
France

1. Place a ready-made pastry crust in a glass pie dish, and bake for 5 minutes at 450°F (232°C). Remove from oven and let cool.
2. Beat 4 eggs and 1 cup (240 ml) cream. Pour mixture into prepared crust. Sprinkle with bacon bits or crumbled bacon. Bake in 375°F (191°C) oven for 30 minutes or until the top is rich brown.
3. Can be served hot, warm or cold.

Garden Frittata
Mexico

1. In a large skillet, heat 2 tablespoons (30 ml) olive oil over medium heat until hot. Add 1 cup (240 ml) each of chopped potatoes, green bell pepper, red bell pepper, shredded zucchini and sliced fresh mushrooms. Cook over medium heat, stirring often, until vegetables are soft, 5 to 8 minutes. Spread vegetables in an even layer in skillet.
2. In a medium bowl, beat 6 eggs, 2 tablespoons (30 ml) milk, 2 tablespoons (30 ml) Parmesan cheese, 1 teaspoon (5 ml) basil, 1/2 teaspoon (2.5 ml) salt and 1/4 teaspoon (1.25 ml) pepper. Mix well. Pour eggs over vegetable mixture in skillet. Prick egg mixture with a fork, and gently lift edges to allow uncooked egg to flow underneath. Do not stir. Cover and cook over low heat for 10 minutes or until eggs are the way you like them.
3. Put frittata onto serving platter and cut into 10 to 12 wedges.

One Dozen Egg Dishes

Deviled Eggs
England

1. Peel hard-boiled eggs. Cut each in half. Carefully remove yolk.
2. In a small bowl, mash egg yolks with a fork. Add 1 tablespoon (15 ml) mayonnaise for each egg used. Stir until creamy.
3. Spoon mixture back into egg white halves. Sprinkle with paprika.
4. Chill. Serve with bread or crackers.

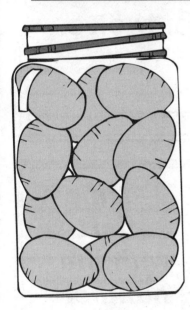

Pickled Eggs
Germany

A simple way to pickle eggs is to place peeled hard-boiled eggs in leftover sweet or dill pickle juice. Put a lid on the jar and chill for three days. Eggs can also be pickled in leftover beet juice. Eggs will keep up to seven days.

Scrambled Eggs
China

1. Heat 2 tablespoons (30 ml) oil in a pan. Add 1 tablespoon (15 ml) finely chopped onion, 1 cup (240 ml) diced ham and/or bacon and 1 cup (240 ml) baby peas.
2. Sprinkle with salt and pepper.
3. Lightly beat 6 eggs and add to the pan. Stir gently over low heat. Cook until the eggs begin to set but are still moist.

Hats Off to

_____

because you know the shape of the number **12**.

Exciting Effort!

You understand the concept of **twelve**.

To: _____

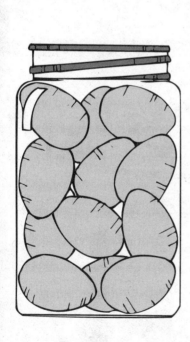

Great work with a dozen!

To: _____

Terrific effort with the number twelve!

To: _____

Counting

One, two, buckle my shoe;
Three, four, close the door;
Five, six, pick up sticks;
Seven, eight, stand up straight;
Nine, ten, ring Big Ben;
Eleven, twelve, dig and delve;
Thirteen, fourteen, maids a-courting;
Fifteen, sixteen, maids a-kissing;
Seventeen, eighteen, maids a-waiting;
Nineteen, twenty, maids a-plenty.

Ladybug, ladybug,
    turn around.
Ladybug, ladybug,
    touch the ground.
Ladybug, ladybug,
    shine your shoes.
Ladybug, ladybug,
    read the news.
Ladybug, ladybug,
    how old are you?
1, 2, 3, 4, 5, . . .

Ten potatoes in a pot,
Take two out and eight stay hot.
Eight potatoes in the pan,
Take two out, there's six to plan.
Six potatoes on the stove,

Take two off and four's the trove*.
Four potatoes in the kettle,
Take two out, leave two to settle.
Two potatoes still aboil,
Take them out before they spoil.

*treasure-trove, meaning a discovery

Counting

Mingle-dee, pingle-dee, clap-clap-clap–
How many fingers do I hold in my lap?
Would you say one?
Would you say two?
Raspberries, strawberries,
Fresh with the dew.
Would you say three?
Would you say four?
Rutabaga, pumpkins,
Onions and corn.
Would you say five?
Would you say six?
Dandelions, crocuses,
Chicory sticks.
Would you say seven?
Would you say eight?
Eggs and cheese muffins
On a dinner plate.
Would you say nine?
Would you say ten?
Then open your eyes
And count them all again.
Mingle-dee, pingle-dee, clap-clap-clap–
How many fingers do I hold in my lap?

One, eat a plum.
Two, touch your shoe.
Three, slap your knee.
Four, touch the floor.
Five, reach for the sky.
Six, pick up sticks.
Seven, look to heaven.
Eight, slam the gate.
Nine, get in line.
Ten, this is the end.

Wink, mink, a pepper drink,
A baby bottle full of ink.
One and one and one are three:
Let's choose sides; out goes he.
Apples, oranges, yellow pears,
Sitting on the kitchen chairs.
Two and two and two are six:
He chooses you; you're the one he picks.

One, Two, Buckle My Shoe

One, two, buckle my shoe;
Three, four, close the door;
Five, six, pick up sticks;
Seven, eight, stand up straight;
Nine, ten, ring Big Ben;
Eleven, twelve, dig and delve;
Thirteen, fourteen, maids a-courting;
Fifteen, sixteen, maids a-kissing;
Seventeen, eighteen, maids a-waiting;
Nineteen, twenty, maids a-plenty.

Write the numbers from one to twenty on the chalkboard. Count to twenty pointing to each number. Randomly point to numbers and let children name them. When students can count to twenty, teach them the rhyme. Break into pairs or small groups of three or four. Give each group a line of the rhyme. Allow time for each group to invent an action for their line. As a large group, share each of the actions. To culminate the lesson, perform the whole rhyme with all of the actions.

Handprint Pictures

Organize this project ahead of time. Begin by reproducing the poem for each child. Attach it to the center of an 11" x 17" (27.94 x 43.18) sheet of construction paper. Provide tempera paint in paper plates or aluminum pie tins. Make sure there is soap and water available for cleanup. Children dip their hands in the paint and put their handprints around the rhyme. When dry, use markers to draw raspberries, strawberries and other objects mentioned in the rhyme around the edges. Mount on heavy paper or light cardboard.

Mingle-dee, pingle-dee, clap-clap-clap–
How many fingers do I hold in my lap?
Would you say one?
Would you say two?
Raspberries, strawberries,
Fresh with the dew.
Would you say three?
Would you say four?
Rutabaga, pumpkins,
Onions and corn.
Would you say five?
Would you say six?
Dandelions, crocuses,
Chicory sticks.
Would you say seven?
Would you say eight?
Eggs and cheese muffins
On a dinner plate.
Would you say nine?
Would you say ten?
Then open your eyes
And count them all again.
Mingle-dee, pingle-dee, clap-clap-clap–
How many fingers do I hold in my lap?

Animal Parade Mural

Review the numbers one to twenty by having students create a mural depicting an animal parade. One animal leads the parade followed by two of another kind, and then three of another kind, etc. For example: one elephant, two lions, three kangaroos. Twenty ants or small animals should be at the rear of the parade. The mural might take many days or even weeks to complete. All the animals should be drawn by the children. Color and cut out the animals and group them in numerical sequence on a long wall or down one side of a hall. When the mural is finished, count the animals. Talk about the animals. Which animals are in front of the elephants? Which animal is the biggest, which is the smallest? Which ones are red? Which animals can fly? Which animals can swim?

Ladybug, Ladybug

Use the ladybug pattern and red construction paper to make a ladybug for each student. Have each student glue black circular cutouts on ladybug's wings. Let children decide how many spots they will use to decorate the ladybugs. Explain that later each will count the spots on the back of his ladybug. As a group, count and discuss the different number of spots on each ladybug.

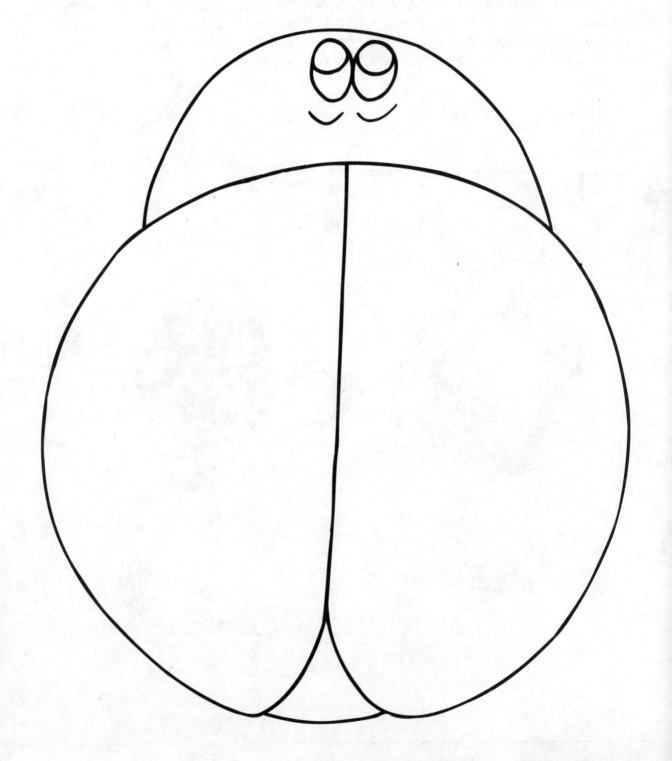

240

Home, Snake, Home

One path has the numbers 1 to 19 in numerical order. Color that path pink.

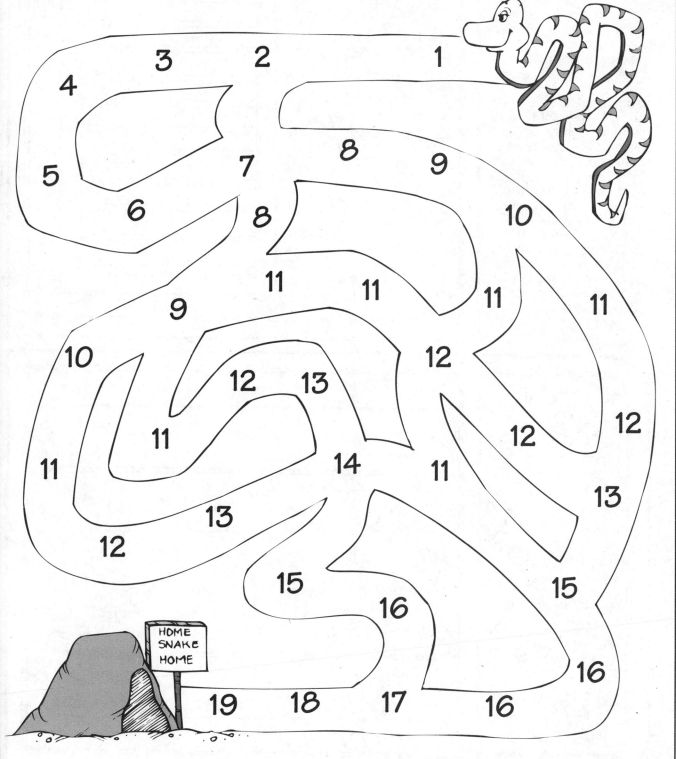

HOME
SNAKE
HOME

Cut and Paste

Cut out the two backpack pieces, front and back. Paste along the sides and bottom edge of the front of backpack and place on the back of backpack to form a pocket. Let dry. Follow the instructions on the next page for the number cards.

Games to Play: Put the books in a straight line in numerical order, or get a friend who has a set of books and turn both sets facedown in front of you. Take turns turning up two cards to make a match. If you make a match, you keep the cards and take another turn. When all the cards have been collected, count to see who has collected the most.

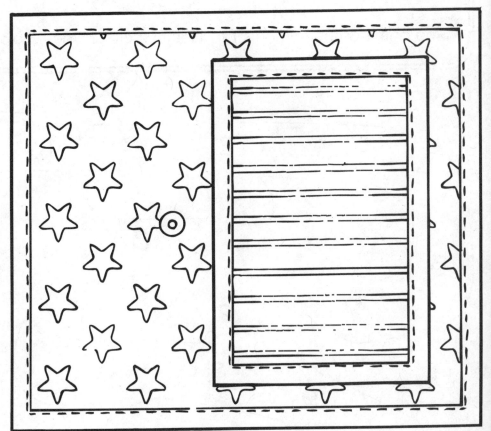

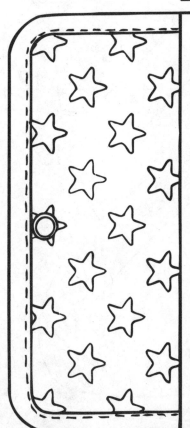

Backpack of Books

Directions: Color and cut out each book. When not using the number cards, place in backpack pocket for safekeeping.

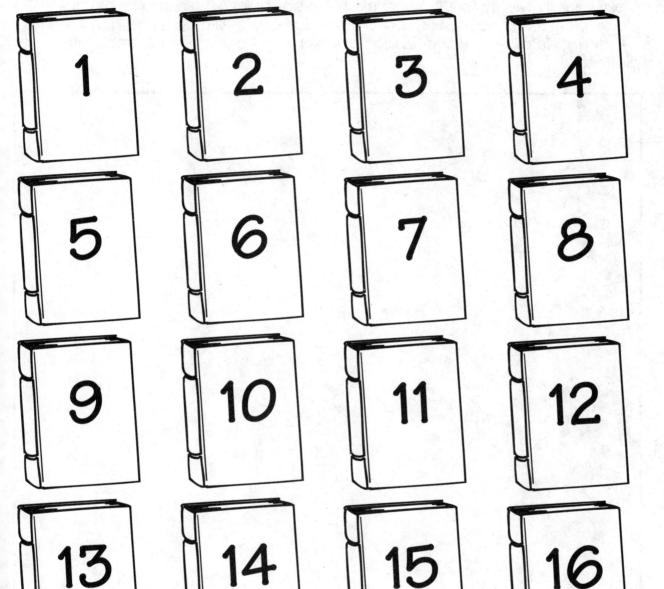

1 2 3 4

5 6 7 8

9 10 11 12

13 14 15 16

17 18 19 20

Counting Thumbprints

Printing with thumbprints is a fun way to reinforce counting. Use a stamp pad to make exactly twenty-four thumbprints in the box below. Use soapy water for cleanup. Examine your thumbrprints more closely with a magnifying glass. Then by adding details with a fine-tip black marker, turn each of your thumbprints into a picture.

Number Numeral Matchup

Getting Ready: Reproduce cards (pages 247-253) on heavy paper or light cardboard. Color and cut apart. For more durability, laminate or cover with clear adhesive paper.

Directions: This game can be played by two or four players. Shuffle cards and deal seven to each player. Place the rest of the cards facedown in the center of players. First player draws a card. He looks to see if he has a pair of cards in his hand. A pair is cards with the same number word and numeral. If he has a match, he lays them down in front of him. Then he discards one card from his hand. The next player can draw the top card on the deck or take the card that was just discarded. There are four wild cards in the deck, and they may be used with any number or numeral to make a pair. If there are no cards from which to choose, the discard pile is shuffled and placed facedown again. The game continues until one player has made four pairs and is declared the winner.

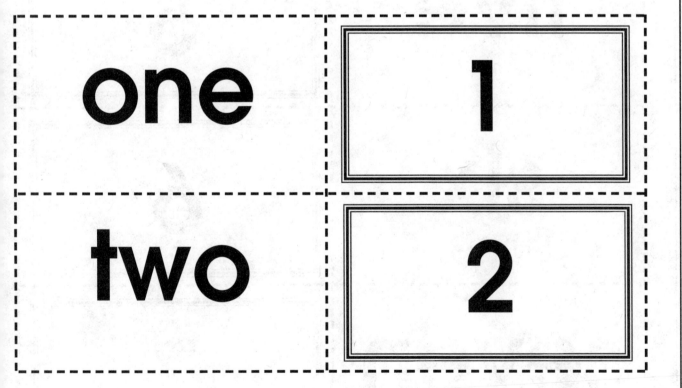

three	**3**
four	**4**
five	**5**
six	**6**
seven	**7**

eight	**8**
nine	**9**
ten	**10**
eleven	**11**
twelve	**12**

thirteen	**13**
fourteen	**14**
fifteen	**15**
sixteen	**16**
seventeen	**17**

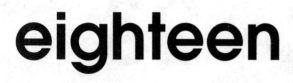
eighteen	**18**
nineteen	**19**
twenty	**20**
twenty-one	**21**
twenty-two	**22**

twenty-three	**23**
twenty-four	**24**
twenty-five	**25**
twenty-six	**26**
twenty-seven	**27**

twenty-eight	**28**
twenty-nine	**29**
thirty	**30**
Wild Card	Wild Card
Wild Card	Wild Card

Counting Games
Ball Bouncing Games

Say this rhyme while bouncing a ball. Bring your right foot up over the bouncing ball at the appropriate place in the rhyme.

One, eat a plum. Put your right foot over. One.
Two, touch your shoe. Put your right foot over. Two.
Three, slap your knee. Put your right foot over. Three.
Four, touch the floor. Put your right foot over. Four.
Five, reach for the sky. Put your right foot over. Five.
Six, pick up sticks. Put your right foot over. Six.
Seven, look to heaven. Put your right foot over. Seven.
Eight, slam the gate. Put your right foot over. Eight.
Nine, get in line. Put your right foot over. Nine.
Ten, this is the end. Put your right foot over. Ten.

While you are bouncing a ball with one hand, use the other hand to perform the appropriate actions while saying the rhyme.

One, eat a plum.
Two, touch your shoe.
Three, slap your knee.
Four, touch the floor.
Five, reach for the sky.
Six, pick up sticks.
Seven, look to heaven.
Eight, slam the gate.
Nine, get in line.
Ten, this is the end.

Counting Games
Jump Rope Counting Rhymes

Use this rhyme to jump rope while practicing counting.

Ladybug, ladybug, turn around.
Ladybug, ladybug, touch the ground.
Ladybug, ladybug, shine your shoes.
Ladybug, ladybug, read the news.
Ladybug, ladybug, how old are you?
(Count to your age.)

One for the money,
Two for the show,
Three to make ready,
And count as you go.
(Jump and count as high as you can.)

Counting Games
Choosing the Leader Rhymes

When choosing sides or captains, use any of these rhymes. Stand in a circle and point to someone as you say each word of the rhyme. The last person pointed to is chosen to be it or leaves the circle depending on the rhyme.

Wink, mink, a pepper drink,
A baby bottle full of ink.
One and one and one are three:
*Let's choose sides; out goes **he**.*

Apples, oranges, yellow pears,
Sitting on the kitchen chairs.
Two and two and two are six:
*He chooses you; you're the one he **picks**.*

Tap Dancing

One, two, buckle my shoe;
Three, four, close the door;
Five, six, pick up sticks;
Seven, eight, stand up straight;
Nine, ten, ring Big Ben;
Eleven, twelve, dig and delve;
Thirteen, fourteen, maids a-courting;
Fifteen, sixteen, maids a-kissing;
Seventeen, eighteen, maids a-waiting;
Nineteen, twenty, maids a-plenty.

Tap dancing is great fun, and counting dance steps is good practice. Even if children do not know how to tap dance, they can learn a few easy steps, and use them to do a little tap dance. Tap dancers click the floor with metal taps on the bottom of the toe and heel of their shoes. Teach the children a few tap steps, and then use the rhyme as a tap dance song. If you have a tap dancer in the class, have her demonstrate and help teach the others the steps below.

Tap Dance Steps

Step: Click toe on floor as you step.
Slap: Slap sole of foot on the floor as you kick foot.
Ball: Place the ball of the foot flat on the floor.
Heel: Without lifting the whole foot, raise the heel quickly and tap it back down on the floor.
Shuffle: Lift one foot and scuff the ball of foot on floor.

Twenty-Five Favorite Flavors

Jelly beans come in all flavors. After reading the list of twenty-five jelly bean flavors to the children, ask them to vote for their three favorite flavors. Graph the results on the board. Discuss the favorite flavors. Discuss the least favorite flavors. Finish the discussion by passing out jelly beans.

25 Flavors

1. lemon
2. lime
3. licorice
4. coffee
5. vanilla
6. raspberry
7. gooseberry
8. strawberry
9. grape

10. chocolate
11. cherry
12. cinnamon
13. peppermint
14. blackberry
15. plum
16. peanut butter
17. spearmint
18. tangerine

19. orange
20. cheesecake
21. coconut
22. green apple
23. pineapple
24. butterscotch
25. bubble gum

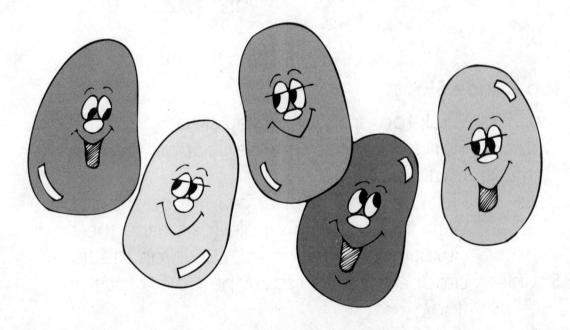

Remarkable!

_____

can count by twos.

All Right!

You can recite many counting rhymes.

To: _____

Congratulations!

You can match the numbers and numerals zero to thirty!

To: _____

Good Counting!

To: _____

Numbers Champion!

To: _____

A little sift, a little shake,
This is how you bake a cake.
A pound of flour, a tub of lard,
See? It really isn't all that hard.
Add some of this and some of that,
Mix it up and pound it flat.
Cook it till it's almost done.
Take it out at half past one.
Now it's ready and time to share.
You go first. I'll wait over there.

Baa, baa, black sheep,
Have you any wool?
Yes, sir, yes, sir,
Three bags full:
One for the master,
One for the dame,
And one for the little boy
Who lives in the lane.

Cross Patch,
Draw the latch,
Sit by the fire and spin;

Take a cup,
And drink it up,
And call your neighbors in.

A Measurement Guessing Game

Cross Patch,
Draw the latch,
Sit by the fire and spin;
Take a cup,
And drink it up,
And call your neighbors in.

Sit children in a semicircle around a table of liquid measuring equipment: teaspoon, tablespoon, ¼ cup, ½ cup, cup, pint, quart, gallon. Have available, two plastic tubs–one empty and one full of water or sand. Show two items such as cup and gallon jug. Record on the chalkboard some estimations of how the two compare. Draw pictures on the chalkboard after each measurement. For example:

Comparisons to Make

1 tablespoon = how many teaspoons?
¼ cup = how many tablespoons?
½ cup = how many tablespoons?
1 cup = how many teaspoons?
1 cup = how many tablespoons?
1 cup = how many ¼ cups?
1 cup = how many ½ cups?

1 pint = how many cups?
1 quart = how many cups?
1 gallon = how many cups?
1 quart = how many pints?
1 gallon = how many quarts?
1 gallon = how many pints?

Variation: Divide class into teams. Give points to correct estimations. Keep track of correct answers, and declare the team with the most points the winner.

Balancing Scales

To make a balancing scale, each child will need a gallon milk carton, two small paper cups, a cardboard crossbar and string.

Directions:

1. Scrub the milk carton and make sure there is no milk residue left inside. Rinse with lemon water and dry. Trim off the top of the milk carton, and turn upside down so that the opening is on the bottom of the carton.

2. From light cardboard, cut out a 12" x 2" (30.48 x 5.08 cm) crossbar. Use a hole punch to put a hole exactly 1" (2.54 cm) from each end of the crossbar.

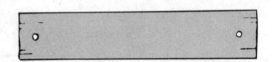

3. Attach the crossbar in the center to the top of carton with a brad fastener.

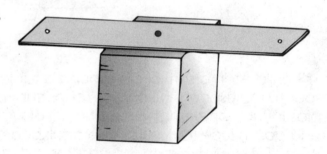

4. Punch holes on both sides of the paper cups as illustrated.

5. Use equal lengths of string to tie the cups to the crossbar.

Provide things for the children to compare weights. For example: coins, pasta, peanuts in shells, erasers, crayons, shells, small stones, paper clips, brad fasteners, plastic cars, craft sticks, etc.

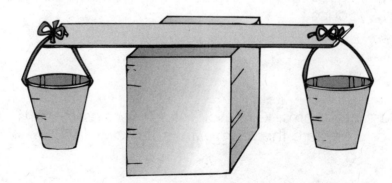

262

Measuring Tools

Make a chart of the things children measure. Show symbols (thumb, foot and yard) and numeric representations. How many "thumbs" equal a "foot"? How many "feet" in a "yard"?

Fancy Foot

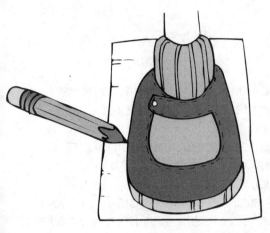

Have children draw around the sole of a shoe that will make a 12" (30.48 cm) outline. Use the pattern to cut out a heavy cardboard measuring tool that is approximately 12" (30.48 cm) long. Encourage the children to use the "foot" to measure the height of other children, doors, windows, desks, etc.

Thumbs Up!

A woman's thumb is approximately 1" (2.54 cm) wide. Cut out a pattern of a thumb that is exactly 1" (2.54 cm) wide. Have the children use the pattern to cut out a heavy cardboard measuring tool. Use this measuring tool to find the approximate length of papers, pencils, crayons, arms, legs, etc.

A Yard of Yellow Yarn

Have students use a yardstick to cut lengths of yellow yarn exactly 36" (.91 m) long. When not being used to measure, children can wrap their yarn on a craft stick. Use this measuring tool to find the approximate length of cars, buildings, playgrounds, basketball courts, etc.

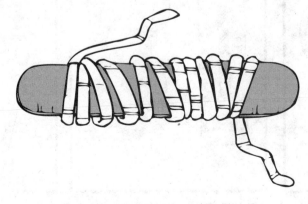

Measuring Center

Baa, baa, black sheep,
Have you any wool?
Yes, sir, yes, sir,
Three bags full:
One for the master,
One for the dame,
And one for the little boy
Who lives in the lane.

Getting Ready: A learning center where children can experiment with different measuring instruments is a good way to teach measurement. Create the measuring center near a sand table or a sink so children will have something available for comparing weights. The center should also contain a variety of liquid measurement tools such as tablespoon, teaspoon, cup, pint, quart and gallon. For weight measurements, include a balance scale, scale that measures ounces and bathroom scales. Provide things for the children to compare weights. For example: bags of coins, pasta, peanuts in shells, erasers, crayons, shells, small stones, paper clips, brad fasteners, plastic cars, craft sticks, etc. For linear measurements, also provide rulers, yardsticks and metric measuring devices. A variety of worksheets or task cards can be placed in the center, too. Encourage students to create task cards for classmates.

Sample Task Cards

Which weighs more,
3 pencils or 10 pennies?

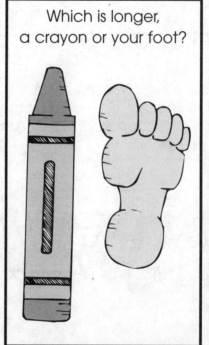

Which is longer,
a crayon or your foot?

How many
cups = 1 pint?

Pick the Longest

Use a red crayon to color the longest worm. Color the shortest worm in the box blue. Color the middle-sized worm yellow. To find out which is the longest, shortest and middle-sized, cut a piece of yarn to match the length of each worm. Then lay the yarn pieces out straight and compare them.

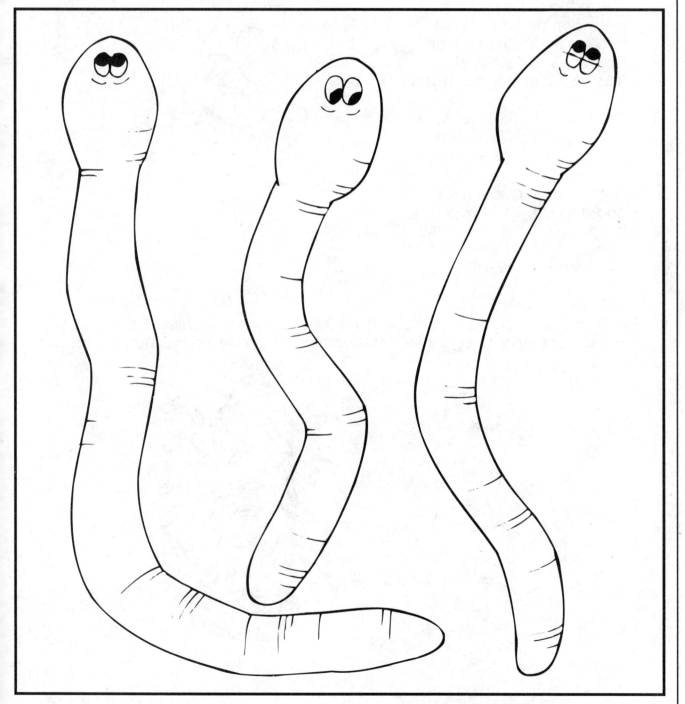

Egg Carton Inchworm

Prepare the egg carton strips for each student ahead of time. Use scissors to cut the sectioned part of an egg carton in half, lengthwise. Cut a 3-section piece for each child. Give each student an egg carton inchworm to decorate. Provide pipe cleaners to make legs and antennae for the inchworms.

How to Make

1. Attach 6 pipe cleaners across the bottom of the inchworm by poking them through the egg carton on both sides as illustrated. Bend back to look like legs.

2. Poke pipe cleaner pieces in first egg section for antennae as illustrated.

3. Cut out large paper eyes and a mouth and paste to the head of your inchworm. Decorate with paper cutout spots, stripes or paint.

How to Use

How many inchworms long is your leg? Measure your arm. Measure your desk. How many inchworms long is the classroom door? Have fun measuring with your inchworm.

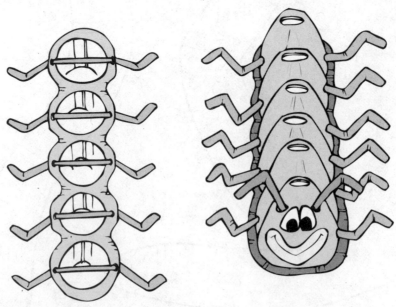

266

Baa, Baa, Black Sheep

Baa, baa, black sheep,
Have you any wool?
Yes, sir, yes, sir,
Three bags full:
One for the master,
One for the dame,
And one for the little boy
Who lives in the lane.

Directions: Use cotton balls to cover each bag. Before you place the cotton balls on each bag, guess how many it will take. Write your guesses under each bag. After you finish covering a bag, count the balls and write that number on the other blank under the bag.

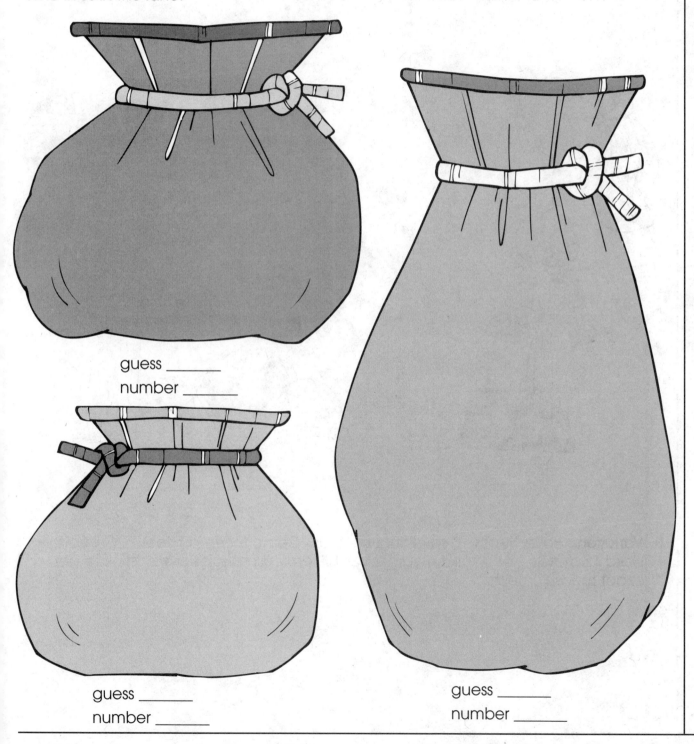

guess _____

number _____

guess _____

number _____

guess _____

number _____

Mother, May I?

Mother, May I? is a good game to play to teach counting and measuring. Divide the class into small groups of three or four each. One person in each group stands facing the others who are lined up about 30 feet (9 m) away. The one who is "Mother" gives the first child a command such as "Take three large leaps forward." Before she follows the instructions, that child has to ask, "Mother, may I?" If she forgets, she has to go back to the starting line. "Mother" gives commands until one of the children reaches the finish line.

Variation: Have "Mother" say things such as "Come forward 5 feet," "Creep forward 12 meters" or "Walk forward 2 yards," etc. Use a ruler or yardstick to get exact measurements.

Brand-New Measurements

Directions: For this dramatic play you will need to have the rhymes on cards with measurement words indicated. Also provide a table of measuring tools such as teaspoon, tablespoon, cup, pint, quart, gallon. Individuals or pairs of children take turns reciting a rhyme and replacing the measurement word with an object from the table. Actions make the dramas more fun, too. When a measurement word is used, the object is lifted from the table and held where the rest of the class can see it.

Cross Patch,
Draw the latch,
Sit by the fire and spin;
Take a **cup**,
And drink it up,
And call your neighbors in.

Cross Patch,
Draw the latch,
Sit by the fire and spin;
Take a **pint**,
And drink it up,
And call your neighbors in.

Baa, baa, black sheep,
Have you any wool?
Yes, sir, yes, sir,
Three **bags** full:
One for the master,
One for the dame,
And one for the little boy
Who lives in the lane.

A little sift, a little shake,
This is how you bake a cake.
A **pound** of flour, a **tub** of lard,
See? It really isn't all that hard.

Chocolate Mini Cakes

A little sift, a little shake,
This is how you bake a cake.
A pound of flour, a tub of lard,
See? It really isn't all that hard.
Add some of this and some of that,
Mix it up and pound it flat.
Cook it till it's almost done.
Take it out at half past one.
Now it's ready and time to share.
You go first. I'll wait over there.

This recipe can be used by small groups or a pair of children to make four large cupcakes. Let small groups of children measure and stir the ingredients for their own cupcakes.

Chocolate Cupcakes

1. Stir together 3 tablespoons (45 ml) butter and $^1/3$ cup (80 ml) sugar until creamy.
2. Add 1 egg and cream again.
3. Add $^1/2$ cup (120 ml) flour and stir until blended.
4. Add $^1/4$ cup (60 ml) Hershey's™ cocoa. Stir until well blended.
5. In a different bowl, put a pinch of salt, $^1/2$ cup (120 ml) milk, $^1/2$ teaspoon (2.5 ml) baking soda and $^1/2$ teaspoon (2.5 ml) vinegar. Stir and then add to mixture. Beat 100 strokes.
6. Pour into four foil cupcake tins, and bake in a muffin pan for 15 minutes at 350°F (177°C) or until done. Cool before spreading on the icing.

Cupcake Icing

1. Cream 1 tablespoon (15 ml) butter and $^1/4$ cup (60 ml) powdered sugar. Stir 50 strokes.
2. Add $^1/2$ teaspoon (2.5 ml) vanilla. Stir.
3. Add 1 tablespoon (15 ml) chocolate syrup. Stir until smooth.
4. Spread on cooled cupcakes.

270

Monumental!

_____

knows how to measure.

You Measure Up!

You understand the concepts
of inches, feet and yards.

To: _____

Fine Work!

_I'm very fond of all the fine
work you have finished with
measurement._

To: _____

Fabulous!

You can
measure in
metric!

To: _____

Fractions

Bye, baby, bumpkin,
Where's Tony Lumpkin?
My lady's on her daybed,
With eating half a pumpkin.

Boys and girls, come out to play,
The moon does shine as bright as day;
Leave your supper, and leave your sleep,
And come with your playfellows into the street.

Come with a whoop, come with a call,
And come with a good will or come not at all.
Up the ladder and down the wall,
A halfpenny loaf will serve us all.

But when the loaf is gone, what will you do?
Those who must eat must work.

Halfpenny Loaf

Boys and girls, come out to play,
The moon does shine as bright as day;
Leave your supper, and leave your sleep,
And come with your playfellows into the street.

Come with a whoop, come with a call,
And come with a good will or come not at all.
Up the ladder and down the wall,
A halfpenny loaf will serve us all.

Introduce the concept of one half. Cut an apple in half, or break a piece of chalk in half. Explain that when a whole is divided into two equal parts, each of those parts is called one half. Recite the rhyme for the class. Then divide the class in half. Count to make sure there are exactly half in each group. If you have an uneven number of children, join one group so it will have the same number of people. Discuss how two halves make a whole. Have half of the children work in one area and the other half in another area. Give each half one verse (half) of the rhyme. Use the picture cues for each verse on pages 274 and 275. The pictures will help the children remember the lines of their verse. Help each group memorize half of the rhyme. Practice. Then let both groups present their half of the rhyme to the other half of the class. In closing, explain that one half can be one thing divided into two parts or several things divided equally into two groups.

Halfpenny Loaf

Boys and girls,
come out to play,

The moon does shine
as bright as day;

Leave your supper,
and leave your sleep,

And come with your
playfellows into the street.

Halfpenny Loaf

Come with a whoop,
come with a call,

And come with a good will
or come not at all.

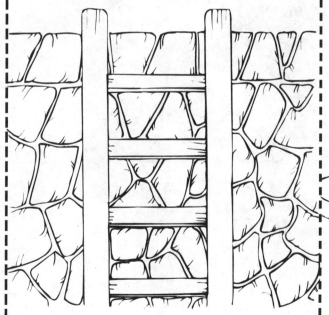

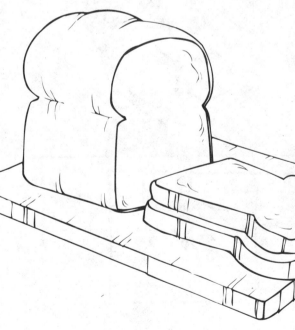

Up the ladder and
down the wall,

A halfpenny loaf
will serve us all.

Craft

Mirror Image Prints

Reinforce the concept of one half by making mirror image prints. You will need large sheets of smooth white paper and black India ink, straws, paints, markers or crayons. Cover the work area with newspaper. Place white paper, smooth side up, on the newspaper. Instruct students to fold their paper in half and work only on one side of the fold. Use the straw to drip small drops of ink on the paper. Teacher should do this for each student. Show the children how to blow through the straw to spread the ink in interesting designs. Before the ink dries, fold the paper in half and press down to print the ink on the other side of the paper. Carefully unfold to see the mirror image of the original ink design. Let dry. Add details and color to the design by using watercolor paints, markers or crayons.

Half a Pumpkin

Bye, baby, bumpkin,
Where's Tony Lumpkin?
My lady's on her daybed,
With eating half a pumpkin.

Color the matching pumpkin halves the same color.

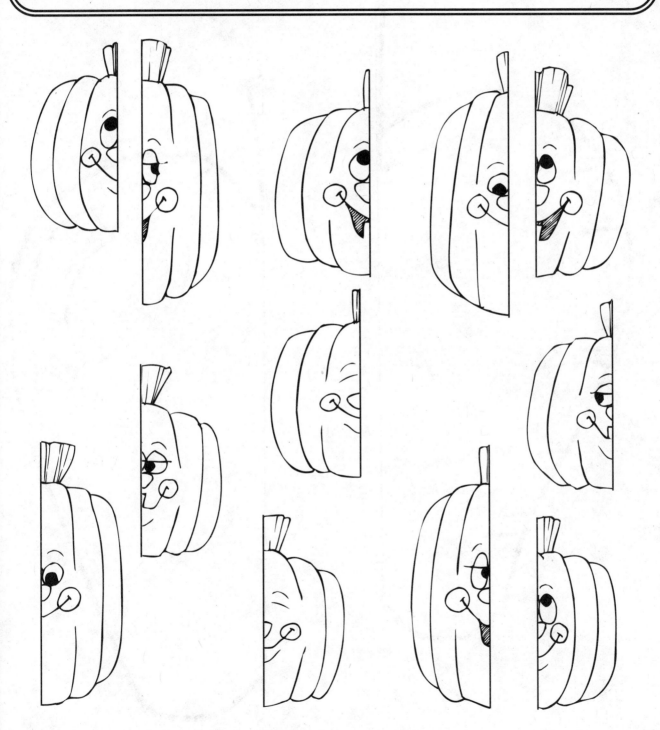

Cut and Paste Fractions

Use the fractional parts below and on the next page to make wholes. Cut out
each. On another sheet of paper, glue the banana quarters and apple halves
together to make two whole pieces of fruit.

Cut and Paste

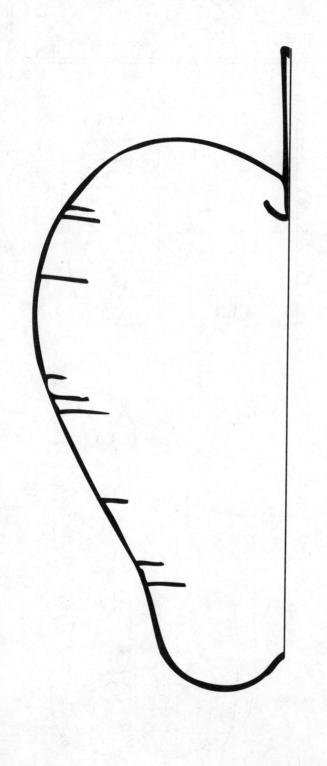

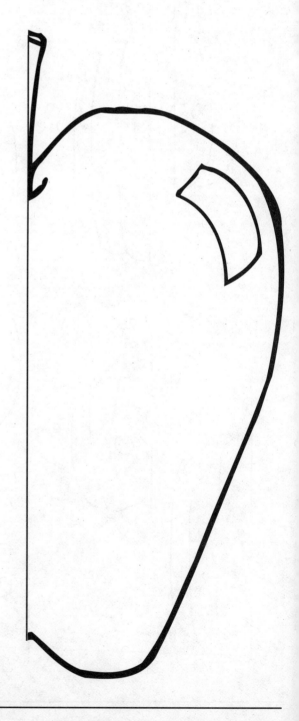

Cut and Paste Fractions

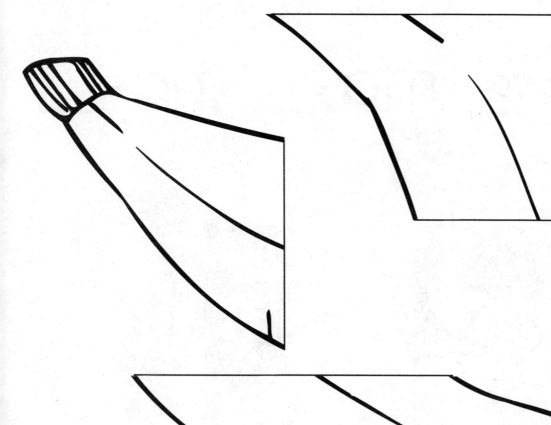

One Half Plus One Half

Here are some words that can be cut in half. The first part of the word is the same as the second part. Write in the second part of each word on the line. The first one is done for you.

yo- _yo_   ma-__   ho-__

bye-____   choo-____

TLC10011 Copyright © Teaching & Learning Company, Carthage, IL 62321

Writing Idea

Guessing the Other Half

Game

Getting Ready: Explain to the children that some things just seem to go together. We think of certain things as half of a pair. For example, peanut butter and jelly, vanilla ice cream and hot fudge topping, hot dogs and mustard or hamburgers and French fries.

Directions: To play this game, the teacher names a food. Children decide the missing half. There are no right or wrong answers. Accept all possibilities.

ice cream and (hot fudge)
apple pie and (cheese or ice cream)
toast and (jelly)
popcorn and (butter)
pancakes and (syrup)
cheese and (crackers)
chips and (dip)
beans and (corn bread)

spaghetti and (meatballs)
bacon and (eggs)
cake and (ice cream)
cookies and (milk)
bread and (jam)
macaroni and (cheese)
baked potato and (sour cream)

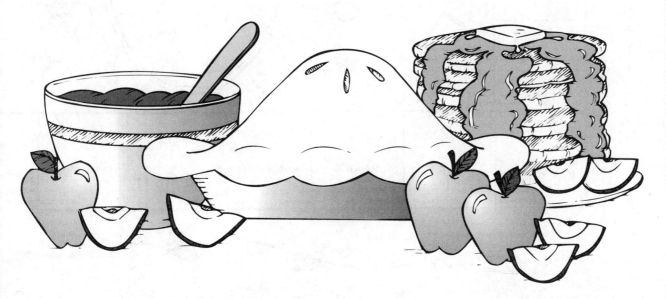

File Folder Game

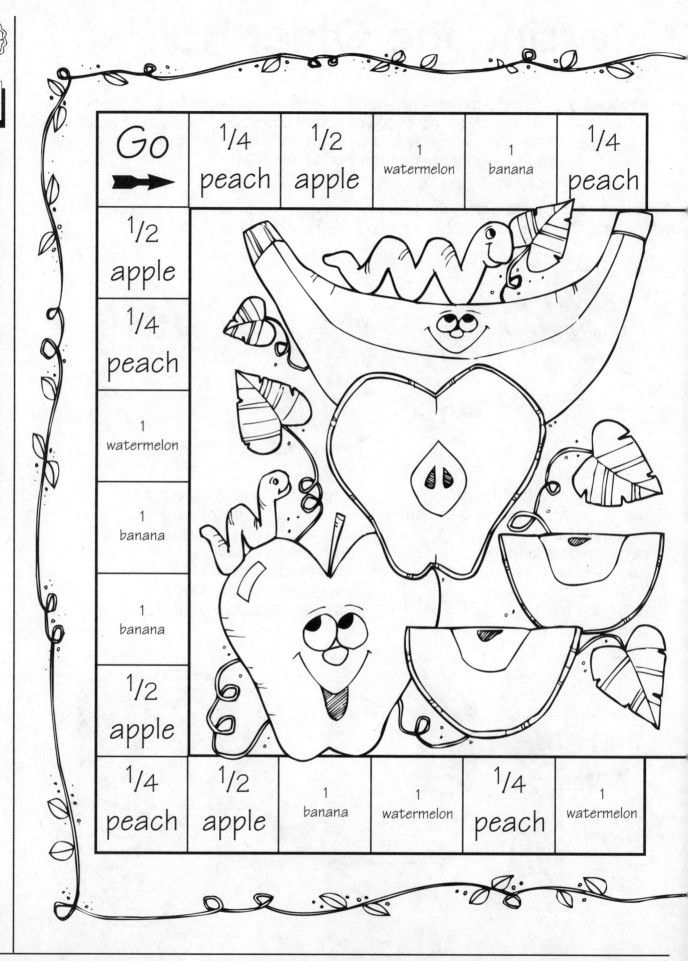

Go →	¹/₄ peach	¹/₂ apple	1 watermelon	1 banana		¹/₄ peach
¹/₂ apple						
¹/₄ peach						
1 watermelon						
1 banana						
1 banana						
¹/₂ apple						
¹/₄ peach	¹/₂ apple	1 banana	1 watermelon	¹/₄ peach	1 watermelon

1 banana	1/2 apple	1/4 peach	1 watermelon	1/4 peach	1 banana
					1/2 apple
					1 watermelon
					1/4 peach
					1 banana
					1/2 apple
					1/4 peach
1/4 peach	1/4 peach	1/4 peach	1/4 peach	1/4 peach	1/2 apple

Matching Halves

Getting Ready: Reproduce pages 284 and 285. If you want more than one game-board, reproduce these pages several times. Attach the game-board halves to the inside of a file folder. Color the board. Cover with clear adhesive paper. Reproduce the spinner pattern below and attach to a half of a file folder. Trim around the edges. Attach the spinner in the center with a brad fastener.

Directions: Children take turns spinning and advancing their marker to the nearest space on the board with the matching fractional fruit piece. The first player to circle the board is declared the winner. To avoid competition, continue playing until every player has circled the board.

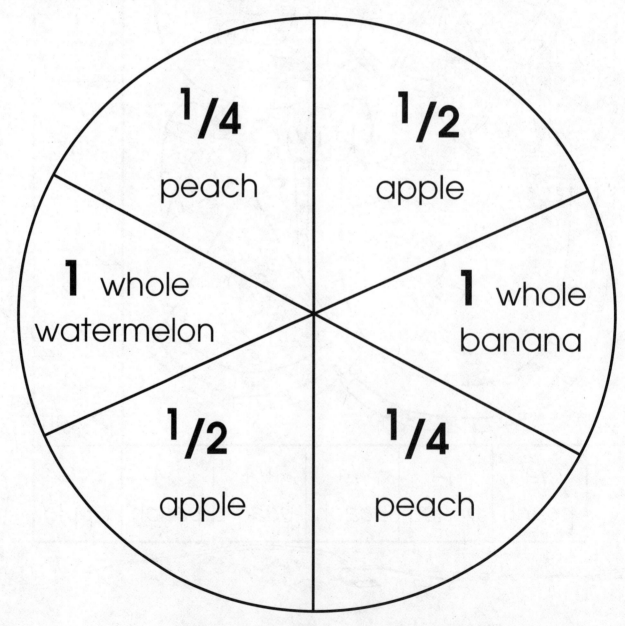

Recitation in Rounds

Boys and girls, come out to play,
The moon does shine as bright as day;
Leave your supper, and leave your sleep,
And come with your playfellows into the street.

Come with a whoop, come with a call,
And come with a good will or come not at all.
Up the ladder and down the wall,
A halfpenny loaf will serve us all.

But when the loaf is gone, what will you do?
Those who must eat must work.

To reinforce the concept of one half, divide the class in half. Have half of the students sit in one area and the other half sit in another area. Practice the rhyme. Then have half of the group say half of each sentence followed by the other half of the group saying the last half of the sentence. Practice one sentence of the rhyme at a time. See if the group can eventually say the rhyme in two sections smoothly without a break in the lines as if spoken by one voice.

Group 1
Boys and girls,
The moon does shine
Leave your supper,
And come with your playfellows
Come with a whoop,
And come with a good will
Up the ladder
A halfpenny loaf
But when the loaf is gone,
Those who must eat

Group 2
come out to play,
as bright as day;
and leave your sleep,
into the street.
come with a call,
or come not at all.
and down the wall,
will serve us all.
what will you do?
must work.

In many countries of the world, fruit is a main part of the diet. Fresh, dried or stewed fruit is often used instead of sugary desserts. For this snack you will need a piece of fruit for each student. A variety of fruit is best–bananas, apples, oranges, peaches, pears, etc.

Fractional Fruit

1. Let each child wash a piece of fruit.
2. With plastic serrated knives, cut each piece of fruit in halves. Talk about the way the fruit looks inside. Mix up some of the fruit halves and see if the students can find the pieces that make a whole.
3. Next cut each half piece of fruit in half again to make quarters. Talk about how many quarters make a whole. Put the four pieces of each fruit together to show a whole.
4. Then let everyone choose four pieces of fruit and enjoy.

Congratulations!

You've done a great job with fractions!

To: _____

Fantastic!

_____

understands the concept of fractions!

Award Certificate

You understand the concept of ¹/2!

To: _____

Fabulous Fraction Award

For the good work you did in the fractions snack center.

To: _____

Good Work,

_____!

You understand the concept of ¹/4!

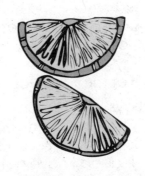

Money

Hot cross buns,
Hot cross buns,
One a penny, two a penny,
Hot cross buns.

Handy Spandy, Jack a-dandy,
Loves plum cake and sugar candy;
He bought some at a grocer's shop,
And out he came, hop-hop-hop.

The king was in his countinghouse,
Counting out his money;
The queen was in the parlor,
Eating bread and honey.

I asked my mother for fifty
cents
To see an elephant jump a
fence.
He jumped so high, he
reached the sky,
And didn't get back till the
Fourth of July.

Simple Simon met a pieman
Going to the fair;
Says Simple Simon to the pieman,
"Let me taste your ware."

Says the pieman to Simple Simon,
"Show me first your penny."
Says Simple Simon to the pieman,
"Indeed I have not any."

To market, to market, to buy
a plum cake,
Home again, home again,
market is late;
To market, to market, to buy a
plum bun,
Home again, home again,
market is done.

Counting Money

The king was in his countinghouse,
Counting out his money;
The queen was in the parlor,
Eating bread and honey.

Before bringing the children together into a large group, assemble stacks of pennies, nickels, dimes, quarters, half-dollars and one-dollar bills. As a group, recite the verse. Count the number of pennies, nickels, dimes, etc. If it is appropriate for your group, explain the value of coins in relationship to other coins. One at a time, have students count a given amount. For example: John, count six one-dollar bills. Juan, count twenty-four pennies. Mia, count seven nickels.

Variation: In small groups, let the children work with coins and bills. They can take turns giving each other numbers of certain money denominations to count. The object of this lesson is to teach children to name each coin and bill.

Famous Me Money

Use the bill patterns to make play money. Reproduce bills on green paper. Children draw or cut and paste pictures or photocopies of photographs of themselves to the center of each bill. Teacher can make photocopies of photographs ahead of time for students. Discuss the value of the bills: $1.00, $5.00, $10.00 and $20.00.

Famous Me Money

These bills can be used to reward students for completing assignments, demonstrating good citizenship or in the learning center (see page 295).

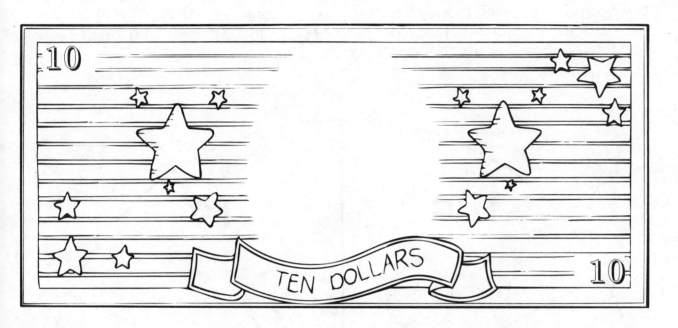

Craft

$

The Countinghouse

The king was in his countinghouse,
Counting out his money;
The queen was in the parlor,
Eating bread and honey.

Directions: Cut out the money ring. Glue to the center of a 9" (22.86 cm) paper plate. Color the pictures. Place on the floor and drop a penny onto the circle. Say the money value where the coin lands.

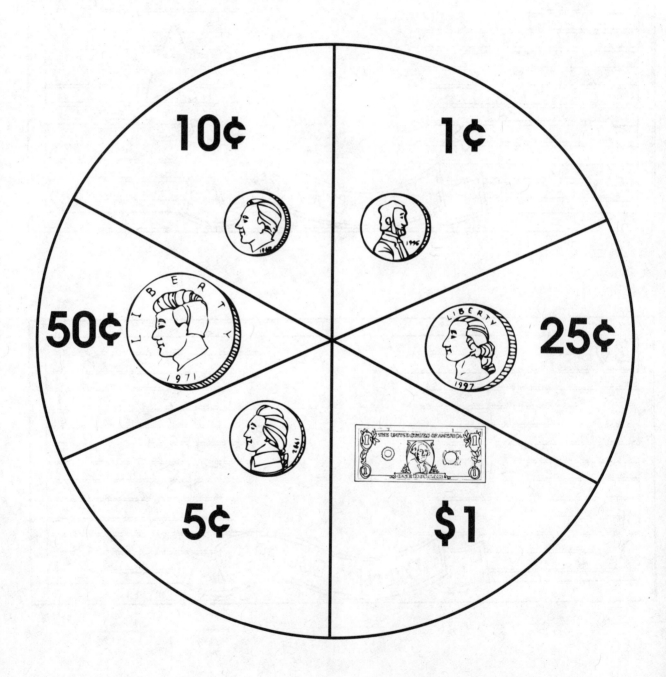

The Supermarket

A classroom supermarket is a good learning center that can be used for many weeks. All you will need are empty food containers, a play cash register, shopping bags with handles and play money.

Getting Ready: Place several bookshelves in the center and put food on the shelves. Place the cash register on a table at the center exit. Put play money in the cash register. In order to acquire the food containers you will need, send home the reproducible note below.

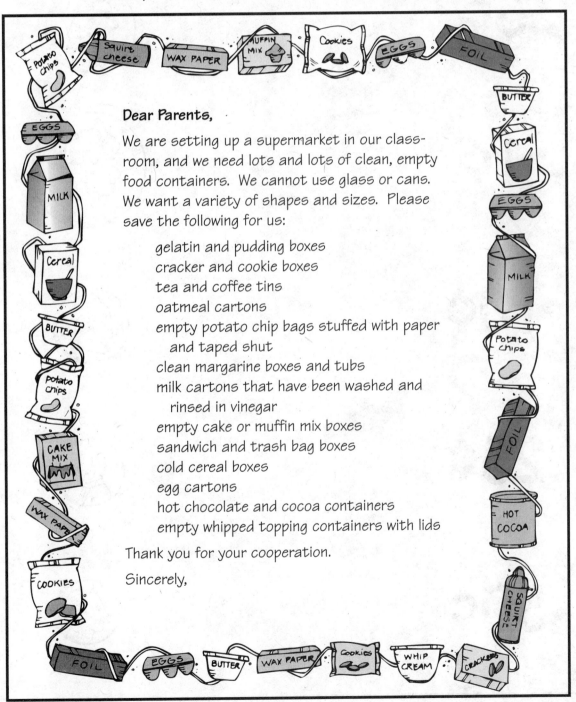

Dear Parents,

We are setting up a supermarket in our classroom, and we need lots and lots of clean, empty food containers. We cannot use glass or cans. We want a variety of shapes and sizes. Please save the following for us:

> gelatin and pudding boxes
> cracker and cookie boxes
> tea and coffee tins
> oatmeal cartons
> empty potato chip bags stuffed with paper and taped shut
> clean margarine boxes and tubs
> milk cartons that have been washed and rinsed in vinegar
> empty cake or muffin mix boxes
> sandwich and trash bag boxes
> cold cereal boxes
> egg cartons
> hot chocolate and cocoa containers
> empty whipped topping containers with lids

Thank you for your cooperation.

Sincerely,

Money Matchup

Draw a line to connect each coin with the correct amount.

5¢

1¢

10¢

25¢

50¢

Buying Plum Cakes

To market, to market, to buy a plum cake,
Home again, home again, market is late;
To market, to market, to buy a plum bun,
Home again, home again, market is done.

Cut out and paste the coins at the bottom of the page in the correct boxes.

25¢

10¢

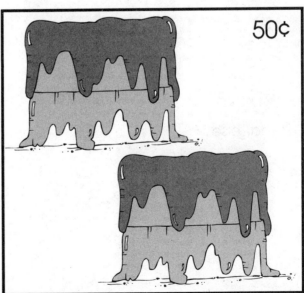

5¢

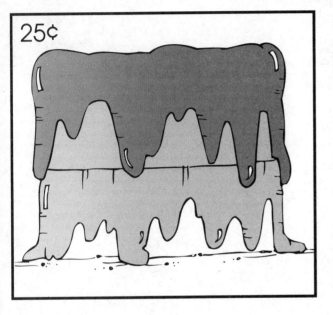

50¢

Writing Money

I asked my mother for fifty cents
To see an elephant jump a fence.
He jumped so high, he reached the sky,
And didn't come back till the Fourth of July.

How many ways can you "write" *fifty cents*? Reproduce the coins on page 301 to complete this activity. The first one is done for you.

1.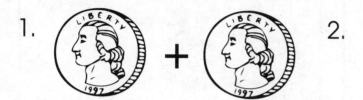

2.

3.

4.

5. What else?

How many ways can you "write" 25¢? 10¢? 45¢? 30¢? 15¢? Etc.

Pay the Pieman

*Simple Simon met a
  pieman
Going to the fair;
Says Simple Simon to
  the pieman,
"Let me taste your
  ware."*

*Says the pieman to
  Simple Simon,
"Show me first your
  penny."
Says Simple Simon to
  the pieman,
"Indeed I have not
  any."*

Getting Ready: Introduce the value of a penny, nickel and dime to the children. Explain that five pennies equal a nickel, ten pennies equal a dime and two nickels equal a dime. It is best to work with real coins when introducing money. Then play a game of buying and selling a paper pie with paper coins.

Make enough copies of the pie on page 300 so that each pair of children will have one. Give each child a copy of the coins on page 301. (Reproduce coins on light cardboard or heavy paper.) Cut out.

Directions: One child is Simon and the other child is the pieman. The pieman holds the pie and tells Simon how much it costs. Then Simon gives the pieman the appropriate number of coins. Then children reverse roles. Continue buying and selling the pie to practice using coins.

Variations: Aluminum pie pans can be used to represent the pie instead of a paper pie if you prefer. Real coins can also be used instead of paper coins.

Pay the Pieman

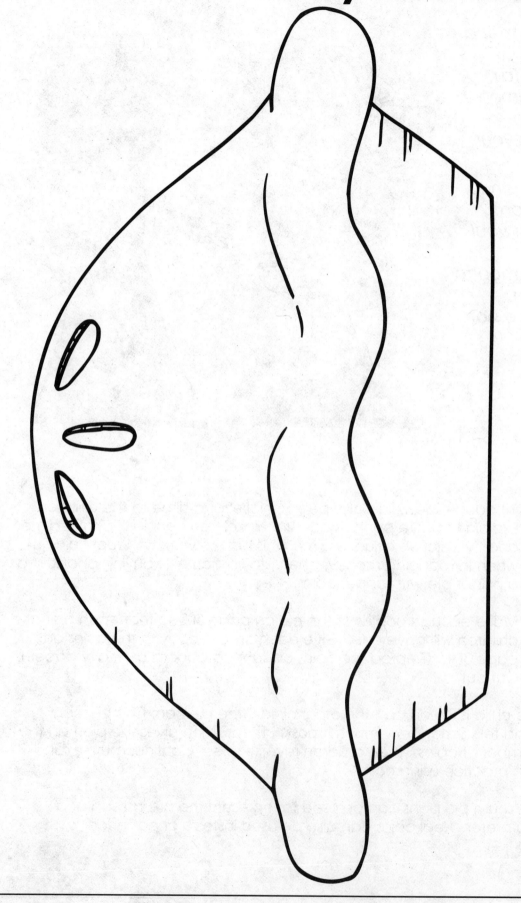

Pay the Pieman

File Folder Game

Pay Up!

Getting Ready: Reproduce pages 304 and 305. If you want more than one gameboard, reproduce each page several times. Attach the gameboard halves to the inside of a file folder. Color the board. Cover with clear adhesive paper. Paste the game rules on the cover of the file folder. If you wish, cover the front of the folder with clear adhesive paper, too. Reproduce enough copies of the coin patterns on page 303 so that each child has three pages. Cut out coins.

Pay Up!

This game is for 2 to 4 players.

Materials:
$5.40 worth of paper coins
one game marker for each player
one red coin

Rules:
1. Place game markers in the "Go" space.
2. Flip the coin to see who goes first. Heads wins; tails looses. If more than one person flips heads, flip again.
3. Flip the coin. Heads move ahead two spaces. Tails move ahead one space. Pay the amount you land on. If you can pay it, you stay. If you cannot pay it, you move back one space.
4. Pass the coin to the next player.
5. Continue playing until you are out of money or until someone crosses the finish line.
6. To avoid competition, play until everyone is out of money and see who has advanced the farthest on the board.

TLC10011 Copyright © Teaching & Learning Company, Carthage, IL 62321

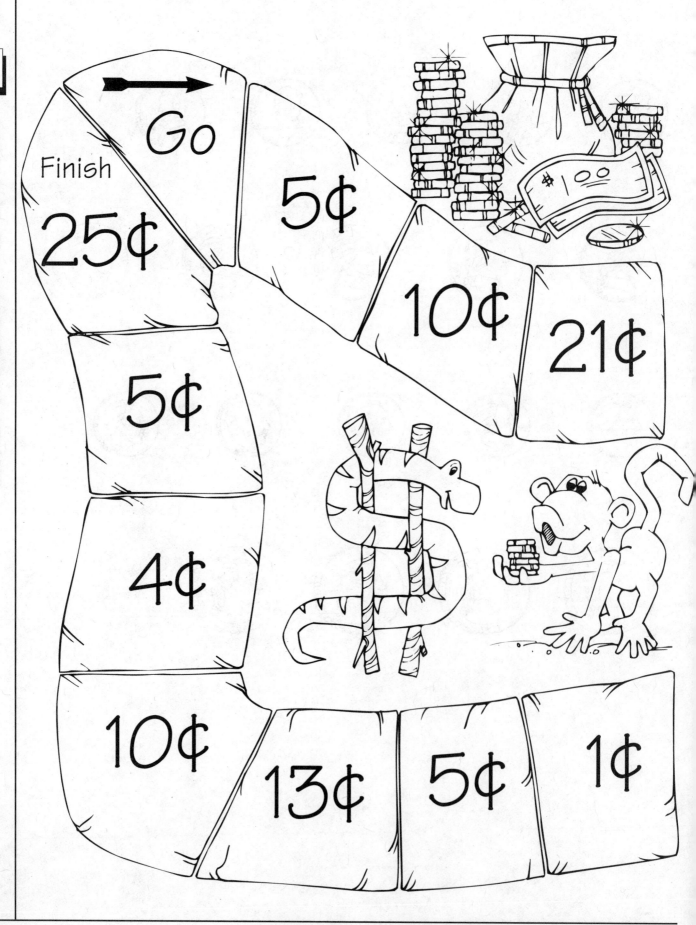

Go

Finish

25¢

5¢

5¢

4¢

10¢

10¢

21¢

13¢

5¢

1¢

50¢

15¢

20¢

4¢

15¢

1¢

5¢

3¢

21¢ 12¢

Marketplace Operetta

An opera is a story told through singing instead of speaking. Operas are usually very dramatic. Explain to the students that an operetta is a kind of opera that is light and amusing. In an operetta, some of the lines are spoken rather than sung. Rhymes sometimes make great songs to perform in operas. To create an impromptu operetta, divide the class into four groups. Give each group one of the money rhymes below and on the next page to perform as a song. Allow children lots of time to practice the rhymes. Then perform all four rhymes as one operetta. Costumes from the Renaissance era will add to the fun. Storefront signs for bakery and candy shops would also be appropriate.

Simple Simon met a pieman
Going to the fair;
Says Simple Simon to the pieman,
"Let me taste your ware."

Says the pieman to Simple Simon,
"Show me first your penny."
Says Simple Simon to the pieman,
"Indeed I have not any."

Marketplace Operetta

Hot cross buns,
Hot cross buns,
One a penny, two a penny,
Hot cross buns.

To market, to market, to buy a plum cake,
Home again, home again, market is late;
To market, to market, to buy a plum bun,
Home again, home again, market is done.

Handy Spandy, Jack a-dandy,
Loves plum cake and sugar candy;
He bought some at a grocer's shop,
And out he came, hop-hop-hop.

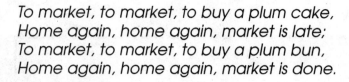

Plums!

To market, to market, to buy a plum cake,
Home again, home again, market is late;
To market, to market, to buy a plum bun,
Home again, home again, market is done.

Plum Buns
United States

1. In a large bowl, combine 2 cups (480 ml) flour, 1 tablespoon (15 ml) baking powder, pinch of salt, 2 teaspoons (10 ml) ground cinnamon, 1 teaspoon (5 ml) ground ginger, 1/2 teaspoon (2.5 ml) grated nutmeg and 1/2 teaspoon (2.5 ml) ground allspice.
2. Mix in 1/2 cup (120 ml) chopped plums, 1/2 cup (120 ml) chopped almonds, grated rind from an orange or a lemon.
3. In another bowl, beat 2 eggs, 2/3 cup (160 ml) honey, 1 1/3 cups (80 ml) milk, 1 teaspoon (5 ml) vanilla and 1/2 cup (120 ml) melted butter.
4. Carefully mix the egg mixture and dry ingredients together. Let batter rise for 5 minutes.
5. Lightly oil muffin tray and spoon batter into each cup. Bake at 350°F (177°C) for 25 to 30 minutes or until light brown.

Plum Cake
United States

1. Mix 1 1/4 cups (300 ml) honey, 1/2 cup (120 ml) raisins, 1/2 cup (120 ml) chopped dates, 1 teaspoon (5 ml) cinnamon, 1 teaspoon (5 ml) nutmeg, 1/2 teaspoon (2.5 ml) ground cloves, 1/2 cup (120 ml) butter and 1 cup (240 ml) water together in a pan over a gentle heat, then bring to a boil and boil for 5 minutes. Remove pan from heat and let mixture cool for 30 minutes.
2. Stir 2 cups (480 ml) flour, pinch of salt and 2 teaspoons (10 ml) baking soda in a bowl. Fold dry ingredients into mixture.
3. Wash and remove seeds from 6 ripe plums. Chop into pieces. Fold plums into mixture.
4. Pour into a well-buttered and lightly floured cake pan. Bake in preheated oven at 350°F (177°C) for 60 minutes or until center is firm and an inserted toothpick comes out clean. Let cake cool in pan for 10 minutes. Best when eaten warm.

Very Good!

_____

knows the values of these coins:
penny, nickel, dime, quarter and half-dollar!

Congratulations!

You know the values of these bills:
one, five, ten and twenty!

To: _____

Monumental!

I am proud of the work you did with money.

To: _____

You Have a Wealth of Knowledge About Coins and Bills

To: _____

Time

Dickery, dickery, dock;
The mouse ran up the clock;
The clock struck One,
The mouse ran down,
Dickery, dickery, dock.

A diller, a dollar,
A ten o'clock scholar,
What makes you come so soon?
You used to come at ten o'clock,
But now you come at noon.

Good horses, bad horses,
What is the time of day?
Three o'clock, four o'clock,
Now fare you away.

Elsie Marley has grown so fine,
She won't get up to serve the swine;
But lies in bed till eight or nine,
And surely she does take her time.

Bell-horses, bell-horses,
What time of day?
One o'clock, two o'clock,
Off and away.

The Clock Struck One

Dickery, dickery, dock;
The mouse ran up the clock;
The clock struck One,
The mouse ran down,
Dickery, dickery, dock.

Look at the classroom clock. Discuss how clocks are used to tell time. Use a gong to strike a certain number of times as children tell how many strikes they hear. Then say the rhyme as a group and strike the gong a number of times again. Repeat to review counting from one to twelve.

Variation: Give each child a small bell or two spoons. Recite "A Diller, a Dollar," rhyme substituting different times in the fourth line. After rhyme, students ring their bell or clang their spoons together the appropriate number of times to indicate the hour.

A diller, a dollar,
A ten o'clock scholar,
What makes you come so soon?
*You used to come at **ten o'clock**,*
But now you come at noon.

What Time of Day?

Bell-horses, bell-horses,
What time of day?
One o'clock, two o'clock,
Off and away.

Recite the rhyme. Then make durable clocks with moving arms. To make these clocks, each child will need a brad fastener and a paper plate with an 8" (20.32 cm) diameter. Reproduce the pattern on the next page for each student. Have children color and cut out the pattern. Paste on the paper plate. You may choose to laminate or cover clock faces with clear adhesive paper. Reproduce the hands below on heavy paper or light cardboard. Color and cut out the hands. Attach to the center of the clock with a brad fastener. Use the clock to practice telling time on the hour.

What Time of Day?

Telling Time

A diller, a dollar,
A ten o'clock scholar,
What makes you come so soon?
You used to come at ten o'clock,
But now you come at noon.

Draw the hands on each clock to show the correct times.

10:00   12:00   2:00

4:00   6:00   11:00

TLC10011 Copyright © Teaching & Learning Company, Carthage, IL 62321

Clock Center

A telling time center will give children the time they need to work with clocks and practice reading them.

Getting Ready: Make several clocks with the clock face pattern below. Glue the clock face to the center of a paper plate. Attach movable hands with brads. (See page 312 for hands.) Also place copies of the time cards from the Clock Concentration game on pages 319-322 in the center. Children can use a paper plate clock to make each time shown on the task cards. Give the children an opportunity to make their own clock to take home.

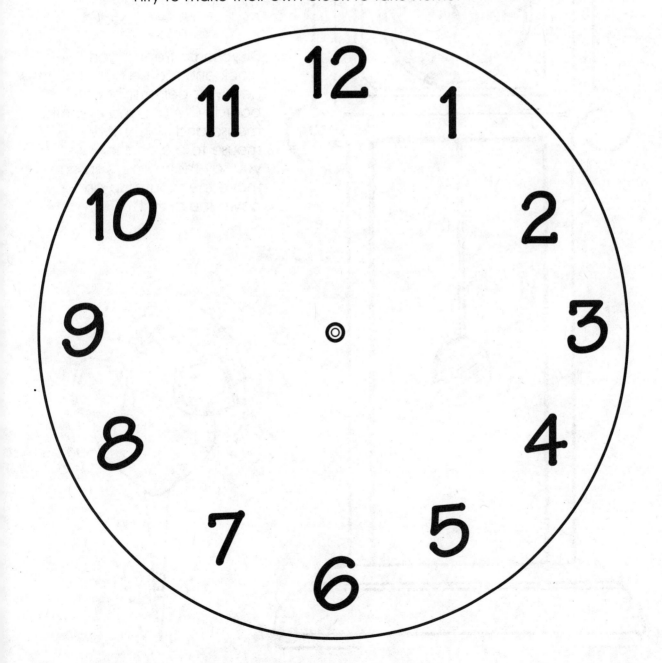

Learning Center

Puzzle

Dickery, Dickery, Dock

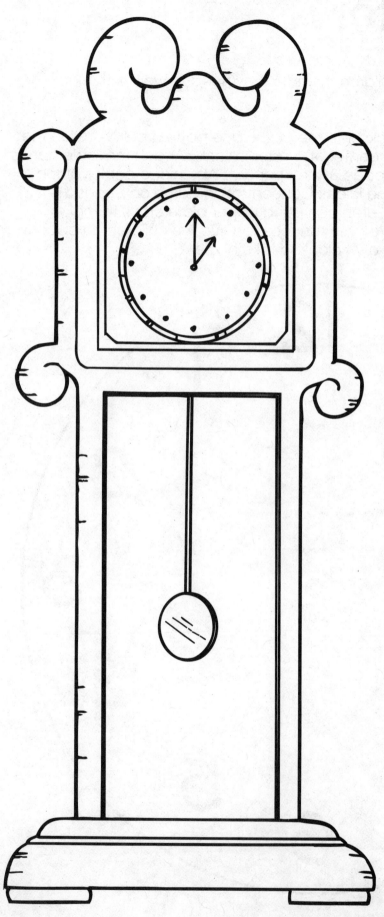

Dickery, dickery, dock;
The mouse ran up the clock;
The clock struck One,
The mouse ran down,
Dickery, dickery, dock.

Directions: Reproduce the clock and mouse patterns on heavy paper or light cardboard. Cut out and color the mouse and clock. Attach mouse to a craft stick. As you say the rhyme, you can move the mouse up and down the clock.

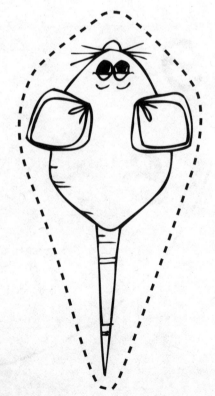

Cut and Paste Clock

Match the numerals and number words, paste the circles on the clock. Color the clock. Cut it out and paste on a piece of construction paper. What time is it? Draw a minute and hour hand to show the time.

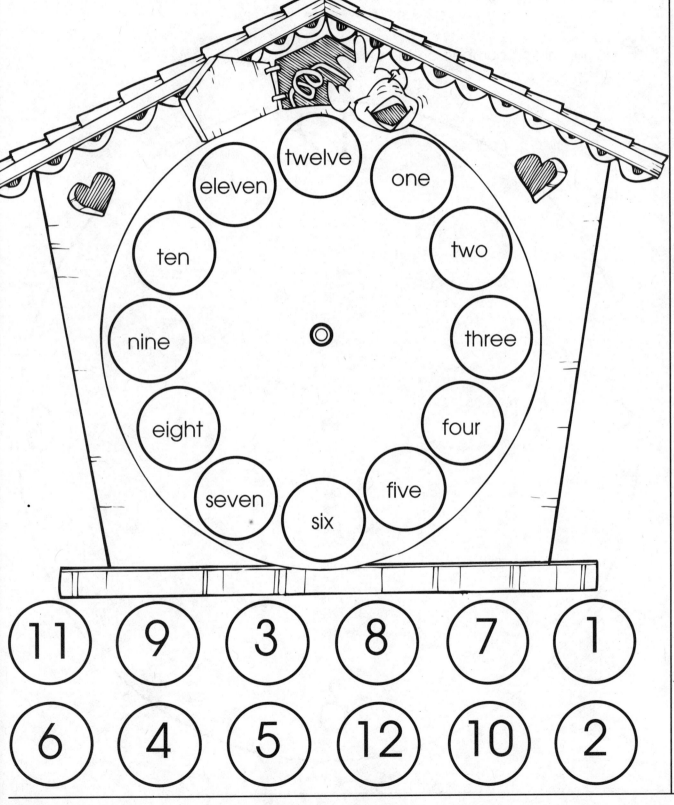

Complete the Clock

Dickery, dickery, dock;
The mouse ran up the clock;
The clock struck One,
The mouse ran down,
Dickery, dickery, dock.

Fill in the missing numbers on the clock. Color the clock.

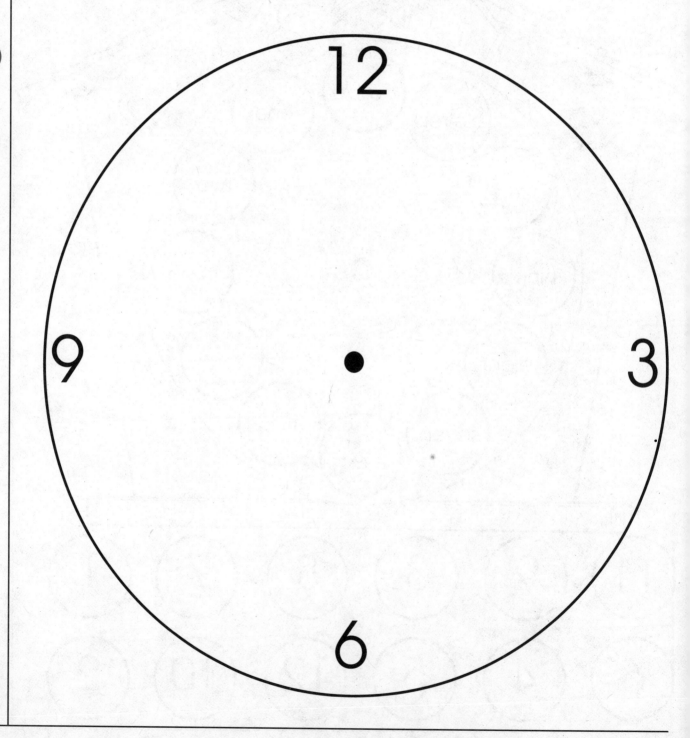

Clock Concentration

Game

12:00

1:00

2:00

Clock Concentration

Variation: Students can use the clock and time cards to play a matching game or to make a booklet of telling time. To make a book, don't cut clocks and times apart. Assemble pages.

3:00

4:00

5:00

Clock Concentration

6:00

7:00

8:00

Clock Concentration

9:00

10:00

11:00

What Time Is It?

Getting Ready: Reproduce pages 324 and 325. If you want more than one gameboard, reproduce these pages several times. Attach the gameboard halves to the inside of a file folder. Color the board. Cover with clear adhesive paper. Reproduce five copies of the clock. Concentration cards on pages 319-322 on heavy paper or light cardboard. Cut out. Cover with clear adhesive paper. Paste the game rules below on the cover of the file folder. If you like, cover the front of the folder with clear adhesive, too.

What Time Is It?

This game is for 2 to 3 players.

Materials:
one game marker for each
    player
game cards
one die

Rules:
1. Place game markers in the "Go" space.
2. Flip a coin to determine who will go first.
3. The first player turns over the top card. If he can tell what time it is, he rolls the die and advances his marker the appropriate number of spaces.
4. Take turns flipping cards, telling time and advancing game markers until one player crosses the finish line.
5. If players run out of cards, shuffle the deck and place facedown again.

Go

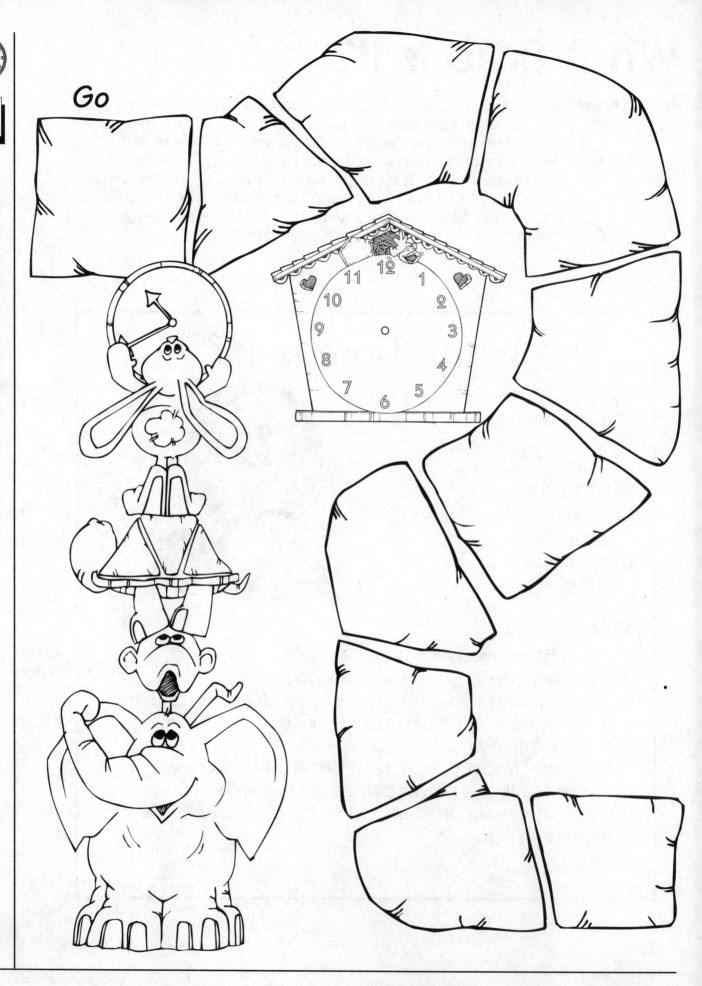

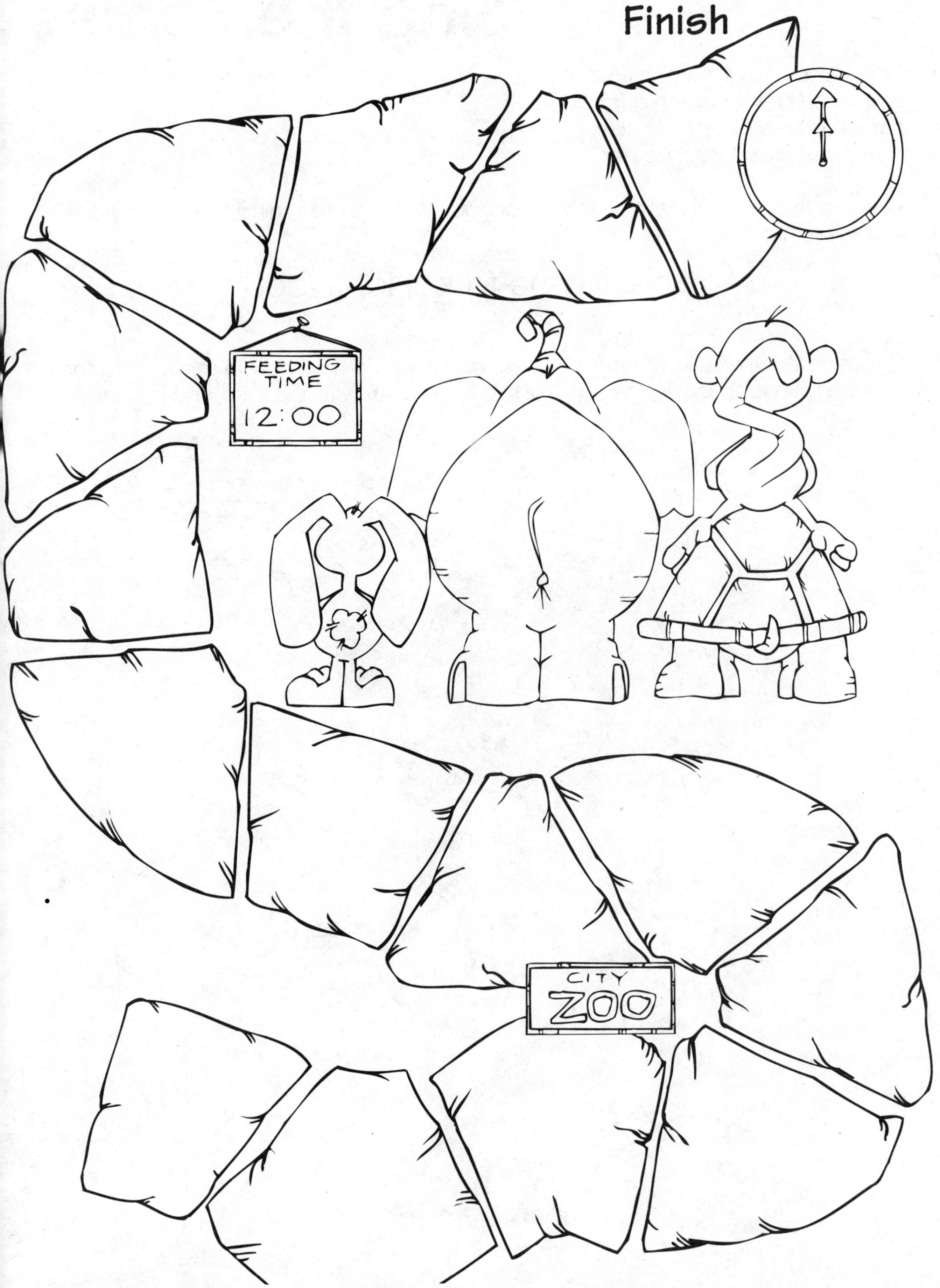

Finish

FEEDING
TIME
12:00

CITY
ZOO

Sing the Scales

Elsie Marley has grown so fine,
She won't get up to serve the swine;
But lies in bed till eight or nine,
And surely she does take her time.

Singing the musical scale is good practice. Begin by teaching the children the scale like this:

Doe, ra, me fa, so, la, ti, doe

Practice the rhyme. Then sing the first line going up the musical scale. Sing the second line going down the musical scale. Repeat with the third and last line.

Oatmeal Time

Elsie Marley has grown so fine,
She won't get up to serve the swine;
But lies in bed till eight or nine,
And surely she does take her time.

Hot cereal wasn't a popular breakfast until the nineteenth century and then only in Western countries.

Oatmeal

United States

Make instant oatmeal and serve in paper cups with a variety of toppings.

milk and sugar	wheat germ
crushed soda crackers and milk	fresh fruit
butter and sugar	granola
maple syrup	brown sugar and cinnamon
chopped dried fruits	sour cream and fruit
chopped nuts	cherry pie filling
raisins	sunflower seeds
jam or jelly	buttermilk

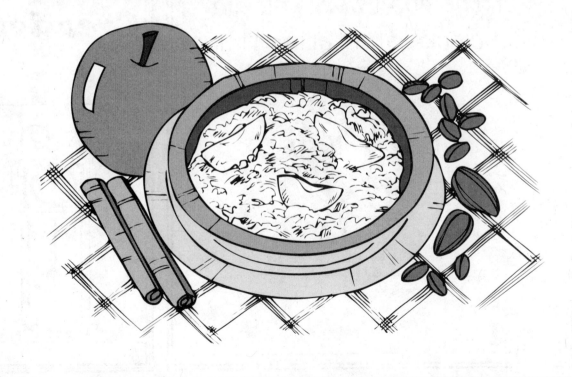

You Know How to Tell Time!

To: _____

Keen!

You understand the order of numbers on a clock.

To: _____

Outstanding!

For the good work you did with clocks and telling time.

To: _____

Clever Clock Creations

To: _____

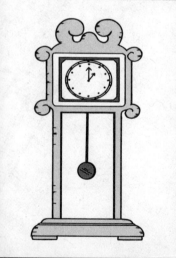